Clean Up on Aisle Earth

Published by 404 Ink Limited
www.404Ink.com
hello@404ink.com

Please note: Some references include URLs which may change or be unavailable after publication of this book. All references within endnotes were accessible and accurate as of August 2025 but may experience link rot from there on in.

Editing & typesetting: Laura Jones-Rivera
Proofreading: Heather McDaid
Cover design: Luke Bird
Co-founders and publishers of 404 Ink:
Heather McDaid & Laura Jones-Rivera

Print ISBN: 978-1-916637-18-4
Ebook ISBN: 978-1-916637-19-1

EU GPSR Authorised Representative
LOGOS EUROPE, 9 rue Nicolas Poussin,
17000, LA ROCHELLE, France
E-mail: Contact@logoseurope.eu

Printed and bound in Great Britain by Clays Ltd, Elcograf S.p.A.

FSC www.fsc.org
MIX
Paper | Supporting responsible forestry
FSC® C018072

Clean Up on Aisle Earth

How Technology Drives Climate Action

Tasmin Lockwood

Inklings

Contents

Introduction

Nothing has defined modern life more than technology and nothing will define the future more than the climate crisis.

Opportunity lies at this intersection. It's an intersection I've explored tirelessly as a journalist, from visiting the labs of a company engineering plastic-eating enzymes in hope of curbing pollution to exploring pilot-scale carbon capture technology at a factory in north London, and covering the legal battle over whether plant-based foods are allowed to carry meaty names. Like many people, I have felt fatigued by the problem. I've also been lucky enough to probe the minds of ambitious founders attempting to build solutions, and that has left me invigorated.

Suppose we wanted to avoid irreversible damage caused by the climate crisis; in that case, we should have acted in the 1990s, when there was a growing consensus amongst scientists that burning fossil fuels would contribute to climate change.

That change has quickly evolved into a crisis. Extreme weather is devastating and deadly: increasing temperatures shattered record after record in 2024, with knock-on effects on health, food security and infrastructure across some US states, Europe and Asia. Droughts have plagued South America and Africa, while hurricanes and resulting floods wreaked havoc on the Caribbean. Damage is accumulating.

Exacerbated by the natural warming phenomenon El Niño, 2024 was the first calendar year on record where global warming surpassed 1.5 degrees above pre-industrial levels, according to the Copernicus Climate Change Service.[1] That makes the chances of limiting temperatures to 1.5 or "well below" 2 degrees Celsius, per the Paris Agreement, look bleak. In fact, a long-term breach of those limits could be locked in as soon as 2028 if we continue to act at a glacial pace.

But, as I've learned over the years, it's not impossible. To get there, emissions must be dramatically reduced – to zero. Many companies and countries have pledged to reach net zero, meaning as much pollution is removed from the atmosphere as is put in it, but the widespread lack of urgency and pace is undeniable. Technology, as a result, can offer a path forward. *Clean Up on Aisle Earth* explores how, through a people and nature-first lens.

I always ask founders, *Why this problem? What was your "aha" moment?* For me, it was when I realised how many litres of water go into making just one pair of jeans – 3,781.[2] The exact figure may have changed over the years as new processes are introduced, but this is what got me thinking seriously about the climate crisis and humanity's unsustainable use of natural resources, and it has stayed with me since. We're facing a water crisis; only around 3% of the world's water is fresh water, meaning it can be drunk, but only 1% of that is actually accessible.

The problem is only intensifying with the race to spin up power- and water-hungry data centres, often in the name of artificial intelligence (AI) and often in countries with scarce water supplies.[3]

It served as a moment of personal reckoning, after which I became vegetarian and later vegan, in the name of the environment. This happened gradually over five years and I share this to not encourage you to follow in my footsteps but to show that change is attainable and doesn't have to be radical. We all have to start somewhere and this is representative of many of the ideas in this book, which navigates seemingly futuristic technology while emphasising proven, scalable solutions that date back centuries.

What if we could "hack" food so that it's more resilient for farming in extreme conditions and increase food security? What if we could accurately predict weather events to evacuate communities, reinforce buildings, and stop hospital blackouts? If we could sniff out wildfires before flames tear through ancient rainforests, burn animals, ruin croplands and spread pollution? The founders of climate technology companies I've spent years documenting believe that we can, or will soon be able to.

Worldwide, they are finding new ways to bring down carbon emissions, mitigate and adapt to the effects of the climate crisis, and provide the infrastructure needed to keep humanity from its worst effects. The shift to renewables is well underway, but many other potential climate solutions are being trialled and scaled up, such as AI to better understand climate risk and industrial-scale plants sucking CO_2 out of the air. Other technologies are still in the lab or are yet to jump off the page, such as those plastic-eating enzymes or "sun cream" to help plants beat the heat.

It is true that much of what we need to solve the climate crisis already exists, "we just aren't politically or ethically motivated to act", as Boston University's director of the Institute for Global Sustainability Benjamin Sovacool told me.[4]

The numbers speak for themselves. Despite the north star goal of zero emissions, we are decarbonising at a fraction of the needed rate. The world cut its use of carbon by just 1.02% in 2023.[5] Cuts need to be twenty-times faster to keep within climate goals, so it's not surprising that we're on track to fly past 1.5 degrees Celsius above pre-industrial levels by 2050 to 2.5 degrees Celsius.[6]

Hitting net zero is just the beginning, given the Earth has many interconnected systems that help it stay healthy. Each has a Goldilocks zone that humans must live within to survive and thrive. If its tipping point is reached, feedback loops could lead to irreversible and unmanageable change. Some may already be triggered, but they are hard to track and constantly disputed[7] – making it even more important to act now.

We often hear that the 1.5 degree goal is dead and that we should move on from it. This is not helpful. While scientists have predicted the goal could be breached, they also believe it would likely be temporary and level out. It goes without saying that the longer we wait to slash planet-warming pollution, the worse the outcome, the more difficult clawing back will be, and the greater our reliance on technology will be.

To Sovacool's point, the energy system needs to be turned on its head. It's currently inefficient and unjust, given the distribution of energy resources. Any alternatives pursued and scaled must be done so in a way that works for everyone, no matter a person's geography, ethnicity, social class or age.[8]

It's easy to feel demoralised by the scale of the challenge, but that's a privilege in itself. Scorching summers in Europe and the US may be a recent occurrence, but they are old news for the billions of people around the globe who have long faced extreme temperatures and weather events. It's especially frustrating when fossil fuel companies continue operating as usual. Exxon has known how burning fossil fuels would impact the global climate since the late 1970s,[9] Shell learned of potential impacts in the 1980s[10] and BP followed in the 1990s.[11] Instead of owning up and changing course, they doubled down and invested in decades-long disinformation campaigns.

Until grassroots movements like Greta Thunberg's Fridays for Future emerged, many world and business leaders failed to grasp the severity of the situation. Still, today, at the time of writing in early 2025, climate action takes a backseat to stakeholder profits. That's why putting a price tag on nature and making people pay for destroying it is essential. Businesses do not typically factor environmental degradation and the value of ecological carbon sequestration, biodiversity or water purification into decisions. Nature simply won't be prioritised if hands are not forced – and money is the language of capitalism. Carbon taxes or pricing mechanisms, which are used to charge polluters for their damaging products and services, attempt to factor in the actual cost of emissions and could give sustainable alternatives a fighting chance by making them cheaper than incumbents. This should also include the social cost, for example, the impact on health and how that is reflected in healthcare systems.

Investment in private tech startups working on climate solutions hit $51 billion in 2022[12] – a drop in the ocean compared with the $7 trillion of global fossil fuel subsidies handed out at this likely peak.[13] Hitting net zero has the same price tag of just under $7 trillion per year.[14] Sure, shareholders of climate tech companies are still holding out their hands for dividends, throwing their real priorities into question: the planet or profit? There are, however, a growing number of exceptions through community interest companies and co-operatives. Even for those in traditional structures, you would be surprised at how many founders acknowledge that capitalism, given its focus on consumption and growth, is the fundamental problem.

Those interconnected systems have a pervasive effect on one another. Increasing temperatures lead to heat-related illnesses and cause the spread of diseases carried by insects such as mosquitoes. Melting ice caps and glaciers lead to rising sea levels, which contributes to coastal erosion. This is compounded by a warming ocean, which harms coral reefs and further breaks down coastline protection, in turn devastating coastal communities who rely on the ocean to eat and work. Elsewhere, water access and quality are reduced by droughts, which also threaten global agriculture and food security. This adds up to a pretty hostile environment for life. Indigenous peoples, whose culture and traditions are often intrinsically linked to land and water, are at particular risk. It also affects migration and resources, leading to conflict and polarisation in an already turbulent world.

The long-established UN Sustainable Development goals reveal how the world must be viewed holistically, with people at the centre. In addition to the Paris Agreement, world leaders agreed on a landmark treaty for biodiversity in 2022, calling for the protection of 30% of the planet and degraded ecosystems by 2030. These goals are possible – global action on ozone depletion in the 1980s shows us what leaders are capable of when they put their minds to it.

What counts as technology anyway? Climate technology is often painted with a broad brush, slapped with a "false solution" label, with critics arguing that it allows polluters to keep on polluting while the planet burns. We must resist this dismissive scepticism, though I admit I do find myself rolling my eyes every now and then. This book is grounded in the idea that technology *can* enable better climate outcomes and enhance nature restoration and protection amidst all of the doom and gloom. The ability to build and innovate out of problems is sometimes considered a mindset of people from industrialised countries, whose economies and businesses are built on fossil fuel extraction. They often did this by snatching land and resources from less developed countries and lower-income communities, which is known as extractivism.

It is a valid criticism. Technology has a long history of exacerbating social issues and perpetuating the systems that created them. Climate tech is no different. Lower-income communities can't afford the high costs associated with home decarbonisation, environmentally friendly goods, or food, which can bolster the class divide. Indigenous communities have practised regenerative agriculture for thousands of years and still do so today, but may be unable to pass on that generational knowledge. Instead, private companies are claiming it as their own. Understanding these dynamics when scaling climate solutions is fundamental in ensuring they are done justly.

Climate solutions face pushback because many are costly and not proven at scale; an overreliance could land us in a sticky situation if lofty promises fall short. Technology can also unjustly allow the world to continue functioning as it is.

Clean Up On Aisle Earth taps into the minds of climate scientists, technologists, investors and activists to imagine life in a zero-emissions world. Many paint a picture where humans coexist with nature and technology, where supportive policies, new business models, and behaviour changes unlock sustainability and justice. Technology got us into this mess, but it can also get us out of it.

Chapter 1
The carbon economy

It's January 2022 and I'm enjoying being a tourist in my own city, Newcastle upon Tyne, curious about its sub-surface history. Armed with a white hard hat and a torch, I stumble down a steep, paved ramp into a dreary tunnel made of clay bricks and sandstone offcuts. Running 85 feet below the surface at its deepest point, the Victoria Tunnel symbolises a bygone era. It was built to transport coal from a nearby colliery to the buzzing banks of the River Tyne, where millions of tonnes were exported annually from 1952 to 2012.[15] There are many tunnels like this around the UK, the birthplace of the Industrial Revolution in the late 18th century. The era brought technological innovations, infrastructure development, vast social change, and, inevitably, pollution.

Before the fossil fuel-driven period that changed everything, the level of CO_2 in the atmosphere was

280 parts per million (ppm).[16] In 2025, that figure stands at 427.09pmm,[17] revealing just how quickly humans are saturating the air we breathe.

CO_2, a potent greenhouse gas, wreaks long-term havoc on the Earth. It lingers in the atmosphere for between 300 to 1,000 years after being emitted, where it traps heat from the sun and contributes to rising temperatures that threaten the way of life as we know it. The world is also experiencing an intertwined nature crisis where many plant, insect and animal species are endangered, pushing global biodiversity into a state of decline. Scientists have dubbed this the sixth mass extinction.[18]

While carbon is the most discussed greenhouse gas, there are actually seven of them. Methane, the main element of natural gas, is also warming the planet. It somehow gets more reductive media coverage as pollution from cow burps and rice fields but also crucially comes from fossil fuel infrastructure via flaring and leaks from wells and pipelines. Methane traps 80 times more heat than CO_2 over a 20-year period but only stays around for 10 to 20 years, meaning slashing methane emissions could be a short-term win for the climate.

Meanwhile, nitrous oxide (N_2O) is emitted through the burning of fossil fuels and nitrogen-based fertilisers in agriculture. In the latter, it depletes soil health, an important habitat for many of the world's species, and contributes to the wider biodiversity crisis. Together, ıane and N_2O are the three most problematic ·arming pollutants.[19]

High- and low-tech solutions

I attended my first tree-planting session in February 2020 as a reporter at a regional newspaper where I observed 19 people plant 100 trees in the name of the climate crisis.[20] Trees use CO_2 in photosynthesis and store it in their roots. When they decay, that carbon is released back into the atmosphere. Healthy forests are known as "carbon sinks" because they absorb more CO_2 than they release. According to one study, forests could sequester around 226 gigatonnes (Gt) of carbon – just shy of a third of the excess carbon emitted by humans.[21] The study also revealed that biodiversity contributes significantly to a forest's ability to store carbon while almost half of the Earth's habitable land is farmland[22] – and agriculture is a leading cause of deforestation.

The Amazon is often called "the lungs of the planet", but the ocean is actually Earth's most significant carbon sink, soaking up 25% of all CO_2 emissions and 90% of the resulting heat.[23] The sheer amount of CO_2 fizzing into the ocean makes it more acidic, harming coral reefs, fish, and the livelihoods of those who depend on them, such as fishermen.

"Climate technology" can today be used as a catch-all term for ancient techniques embedded in nature, split between "nature-based" or "low-tech" solutions, as well as more modern methods, known as "engineered" or "high-tech" solutions. Some innovators are working at their intersection with tech used to enhance, enable and speed up beneficial natural processes. Others are identifying ways to fund nature protection and restoration to create new business models, including for existing, zero-emissions technologies that support this goal. The community project I visited in 2020, for example, was seeking grant funding, a typical and important route for environmental projects, but wholly inadequate for the eye-watering scale that's needed to make a dent in the climate crisis.[24]

Many high-profile scientists, activists and investors believe resources are best spent scaling up proven technologies, like solar, wind and heat pumps. Novel technology is often labelled a distraction, a false fix that steers money away from genuine, long-term solutions. In contrast, proponents claim that technology will be needed to undo historical damage as even if all emissions were suddenly stopped today, some climate change is permanent. These arguments are not mutually exclusive.

A popular analogy asks you to imagine you've been filling a bathtub for a while and it's about to overflow. What do you do? You turn off the tap *and* you pull the plug to let some water out. The atmosphere is the bathtub and the water is the concentration of CO_2. We must adopt this two-pronged approach in actuality.

Pulling the plug to remove carbon has some heavy-hitting supporters with Microsoft, Google's Alphabet, Facebook's Meta and payment company Stripe supporting the industry through Frontier, a pioneering $1 billion advanced market commitment designed to nurture nascent technology. Its investments span a portfolio of different removals including nature and high-tech solutions.[25]

However, it is a tiny part of the picture. The bath tap also needs to be turned off: emissions must be slashed across the global food and energy systems, the urban environment, supply chains and everything in between. A host of fixes do exist but if *this much* needs to be changed, it begs the question: what is systematically going wrong? These technologies don't tackle the underlying issues that have led to this mess.

Electric vehicles (EV) are a good example, which ultimately haven't threatened our established way of life. Investing in public transport[26] and electrifying it would make more sense[27], since private car ownership is often unnecessary and perpetuates class divides. EV batteries are troublesome, as they need mined materials typically found in the Global South, where labour issues also occur.[28] Wealthy countries, typically in the Global North, drive demand for these materials and critics argue that their extraction should be considered neocolonialism. They are also difficult to recycle and can harm the environment by leaking toxic chemicals when discarded.

Instead of drop-in alternatives such as this, we need a complete overhaul, but a personal car ban, for example, would be radical. To reach critical mass, we need the masses; this has embolised action and led us into an uneasy dance between protecting the planet and human agency. Technologists and policymakers must pay careful attention to this, ensuring a fair balance is found. As the twentieth-century philosopher Isaiah Berlin warned: "Freedom for the wolves has often meant death to the sheep."

Whether it's restoring forests, new energy infrastructure or sucking carbon from out of the atmosphere, any solution that wants to stand the test of time needs to have community buy-in from those who are affected by it. Mirroring the actions of extractivist industries they're designed to replace, green projects have sometimes ploughed ahead without such consideration. Indigenous communities in Cambodia have been evicted from their ancestral lands for carbon offset projects;[29] Scottish farmers have hit back at plans to put pylons through their land, claiming it will make it difficult to work;[30] and one neighbourhood in Medellin, Colombia, faced job losses and worries of displacement due to climate measures.[31]

Meaningful engagement isn't just the right thing to do, it also makes financial sense. Researchers have found that a lack of consultation and dialogue can lead to greater opposition and, therefore, delays.[32] Those who go ahead often do so after hefty investments in resolutions, making it more cost and time-efficient to work with communities from the get-go.

The whole process could be flipped on its head. Project Drawdown, a non-profit focused on furthering climate action, puts 6% of potential emissions reductions down to "people first and planet second" interventions.[33] By protecting people *and* nature, emissions reductions will come as a byproduct, rather than vice versa. I saw this first-hand in the Bolivian part of the Amazon Rainforest when I was backpacking around Latin America and also writing this book. The trip was born out of a compulsion to see the rainforest before it (I cynically joke, pleading it not to be true) is completely destroyed. I hope we never get to that point, of course, but the fire and logging risks it faces are persistent. Ironically, even COP, the UN's Conference of the Parties where world leaders meet annually to discuss climate policy, led to deforestation in the Brazilian Amazon,[34] as the country prepped to host the 2025 rendezvous.

According to my local guide during the trip, sustainable tourism gives Indigenous communities in Madidi National Park a way to make money and continue practising traditional skills, alleviating pressure to sell land.

Carbon removal spans the gamut

Carbon removal is becoming more important as the world fails to slash emissions quickly enough. Scientists believe we will need up to 9 gigatons of CO_2 removed from the atmosphere annually by 2050.[35] This figure currently stands at just 2 billion tons per year today, with nature doing the heavy lifting. Supporters of carbon removal often cite that the Intergovernmental Panel on Climate Change (IPCC)'s pathways all include some element of it. However, there are cautionary notes throughout the IPCC's work against a reliance on "speculative technologies".[36]

Twin targets of emissions reductions and carbon removals are one way of moving away from the question of technology being a moral hazard, and are championed by the likes of Ben Rubin, executive director of industry coalition the Carbon Business Council.[37] They could bring more transparency to the market, help beat the perception that carbon removal is a substitute for urgently needed emissions cuts, prevent the divisive either-or mindset and, according to Rubin, highlight the fact that both levers must be pulled at the same time if we want to address climate change today *and* tomorrow.

Sucking carbon out of the air

Lying just west of Iceland's capital Reykjavík, Hellisheiði is a lava plateau known for its sizable geothermal power plant. Formed volcanically, the underground geothermal activity makes the perfect setting for energy-intensive industries that want to tap into abundant energy. Hellisheiði is also the home to the world's most significant direct air capture and storage plant operated by the startup Climeworks, which opened in May 2024.

Direct air capture (DAC) uses chemical processes to capture CO_2 directly from ambient air, which is then used for storage or utilisation. The Mammoth plant has the capacity to capture 36,000 tons of CO_2 per year,[38] about ten times the size of its sibling Orca, Climeworks' first plant, but its success is a lingering question.[39] It's common for new technologies to experience teething problems but DAC is a tough sell given the process is incredibly energy-intensive, which is criticised by some climate scientists, such as Stanford professor Mark Jacobson.[40] He argues that switching a fossil fuel plant to renewable energy is far more effective in reducing emissions than using that same renewable energy to power a DAC plant. "Compared with transitioning to clean, renewable energy, carbon capture and direct air capture are opportunity costs that increase carbon dioxide, air pollution, energy needs, and energy costs," he told me, pointing to a research paper that made the same statement.[41]

There are concerns that any kind of technology-driven carbon capture allows for continued pollution but this is where politicians should step in, to ensure that it is only used for historic emissions. Huge, centralised industrial plants are a far-cry from a people-first transition, given they offer few benefits beyond jobs. Instead, they take up limited land and can increase air pollution.[42]

Given the renewable energy demands and specific geology needed for DAC and storage, companies typically originating in the Global North are eyeing previously overlooked areas to set up shop, a dynamic that could be capitalised on and uplift struggling communities if the right terms are found. For example, Kenyan organisation Great Carbon Valley is campaigning to bring DAC and other energy-intensive industries to the country, where nearly 90% of the grid is renewable or clean energy.[43] While energy is plentiful, it's expensive, and developers are hesitant to build new projects without guaranteed buyers so the country's potential remains untapped, Great Carbon Valley CEO Bilha Ndirangu told me.[44]

The organisation aims to build green industrial sites that combine renewables with industries like DAC, which it is particularly well-suited to due to its underground geology. It also plans to co-locate renewable energy projects with such companies, ideally cutting the cost of energy due to the lack of grid connection and transmission fees. How does that help Kenyans? While surplus energy could be sold to locals, DAC has the potential to bring jobs, industry, and cheaper energy.

While still a nascent sector, governments are bullish. Under Joe Biden, the US Government was pursuing a $3.5 billion DAC hub programme to encourage similar facilities to spin up across the US. Amid a second Donald Trump presidency, which has halted and gutted much of the US' climate initiatives, the programme's fate is uncertain.[45] Trump did confirm a tax credit for DAC in the One Big Beautiful Bill Act but storing captured carbon geologically or using it to extract oil in enhanced oil recovery are equally incentivised.[46]

Job creation is really at the core of governmental climate tech investment, regardless of whether it's in Kenya or the US. The idea is that spending will trickle down to marginalised communities hit hardest by the impacts of the climate crisis, pollution and job losses related to the oil and gas industry. In the US, that has actually started to happen.[47]

The UK, Canada, and Japan are also backing the use of DAC as part of a wider carbon capture, utilisation, and storage play. However, utilisation is where things get more murky; the carbon is still eventually returned to the atmosphere but it is recycled and reused in the meantime, which could be a sweet deal for the likes of food and beverage companies who make carbonated drinks – if the price is right.

Stopgap solutions

There is sometimes conflation between carbon capture and carbon removal. Carbon capture is the retrofitting of technology onto polluting systems, such as the smokestacks on a ship or fossil-fuelled power plants, to stop CO_2 from entering the atmosphere. These stopgap systems allow polluters to keep operating business as usual, which is convenient for the fossil fuel industry. However, proponents argue they play an essential role in cutting emissions from systems or sectors that are hard to transition away from fossil fuels, such as steel and cement production, which are often referred to as "hard to abate".

Carbon capture has been used for enhanced oil recovery since the 1960s,[48] where captured carbon is injected into wells to push out crude oil. That's how the paradoxical idea of "net zero oil" emerged, because carbon is stored as more oil is extracted. As of 2021, 73% of captured carbon is used for enhanced oil recovery.[49] However, permanent storage is set to overtake enhanced oil recovery by 2030 thanks to legislation that favours storage over captured carbon utilisation.

It's easy to see how the fossil fuel industry's embrace of carbon capture and DAC would allow them to avoid accountability. Many oil and gas majors claim to have progressive climate targets but they actually only apply to a portion of their emissions, excluding those in their supply chain.[50] Thus, they completely avoid the pollution associated with burning the products they extract and sell. Direct air companies such as Climeworks and its US peer Heirloom Carbon have long maintained that they wouldn't work with oil and gas companies for enhanced oil recovery. High-tech carbon removal should be a final strategy after decarbonisation.

I covered climate tech during an investment boom in 2021 when the startup scene was abuzz. Founders, promising to change and save the world, raised millions at speed. Technology may dominate our everyday lives but, applied to climate, it is a tiny and novel industry. In that lies a considerable criticism – and opportunity. Why pump billions into a risky ploy when we could be investing in forests and mangroves? Well, we need both. Carbon removal isn't unique in needing colossal amounts of capital to reach and be proven at the scale it needs to be.

Investors are torn. The energy costs of DAC are difficult to reconcile, thus throwing its role in an emissions-free future into doubt. One of the biggest draws is that it's easy to measure how much CO_2 has actually been captured as it's in the device, which actually removes some level of risk and contrasts nature-based approaches.

There is more consensus on carbon capture: it will play a part, though the social licence is more difficult to obtain as it's seen as a technology that avoids necessary transitioning. Building a sustainable world should involve deconstructing the systems that led us to this sorry state; simply capturing emissions before they are released but still allowing fossil fuels to be extracted and used is not good enough.

How significant a role any of these carbon removal technologies will be is still to be seen. Success may come down to marketing and community engagement, as anyone pursuing novel technologies needs a strong social mandate to operate.[51] Restoring nature is a much easier sell.

Natural wins

In a 2014 NASA time-lapse of how emissions sweep around the Earth every year, deep red and purple plumes representing CO_2 engulf the northern hemisphere through winter.[52] In summer, as plants all bloom and grow, the dark colours dissipate, representing the constant ebb and flow between seasons. Harmful carbon monoxide, a product of fires ravaging the southern hemisphere, appears. Neither gas stays where it's emitted but instead travels with the wind. When the time-lapse ticks back to winter, as biomass dies and releases methane, the red gas returns. Nature *can* regulate the climate, if we just give it a chance.

Tree planting typically comes to mind when I hear "nature-based solutions". The 19 locals I watched break soil in 2020 are far from alone in their mission: communities, companies and countries are working together globally to restore and conserve the planet. 1t.org, for example, is a lofty initiative to help corporations "conserve, restore and grow a trillion trees by 2030 for people, biodiversity and planet".[53]

Reforestation refers to actions that protect, manage and restore ecosystems on land and in the ocean. Good reforestation projects can include restoring forests, peatlands and coastal ecosystems.

But projects aren't always good. Using carbon as a measurement has encouraged huge, fast-growing monocultures where just one species is planted to maximise carbon stores, rather than to create diverse ecosystems that are found in the natural world. Monocultures have limited benefits to biodiversity and are far more vulnerable to disease, creating trouble for the environment, especially when it comes to food production.

Sometimes, rich forests are cut down and saplings are planted elsewhere as an exchange, but the scale of loss is far greater than face value. It takes decades to establish a mature ecosystem that is home to rich biodiversity and can lock up large amounts of CO_2. The case for preserving existing ecosystems, known as avoiding deforestation, is a no-brainer and the numbers are clear: land use change, mainly deforestation, was responsible for up to 20% of global greenhouse gas emissions as of 2020.[54]

The snag is when there's a financial incentive for protecting threatened forests and cowboy conservationists emerge. It's difficult to prove when a forest is at risk, throwing the impact of preservation into question. Deforestation can even be incentivised ahead of initial risk assessments so that impact results are skewed – a bigger impact equals a bigger payday. This speaks to how a narrow focus on carbon can do more harm than good, especially when it comes to biodiversity. There are countless initiatives and monitoring technologies designed to reduce these risks and operators with mal intent accountable but the system is imperfect.

Conservation projects have also been known to restrict access to communities who may have deep, ancestral connections to the land and rely on it for hunting or medicinal plants. Indigenous peoples, who comprise a small percentage of the world's population, are believed to protect 80% of its biodiversity through their ancestral land.[55] They also make up nearly one-fifth of the world's extreme poor.[56] As I learned in the Amazon Rainforest in 2024, some communities are under pressure from private interests that want to exploit land for mining[57] and the expanding agriculture frontier.[58] Selling it for parts or converting to cattle-led agriculture might be some families' only source of income. There will be no green transition until we recognise these and other challenges around work and poverty. People of every ilk – Indigenous communities to oil and gas veterans affected by industry job losses – must be brought along rather than chastised.

Many technologies are being used to help monitor, map, restore, measure and verify nature and the effects of interventions. Sensors, high-powered satellites and aerial surveys track complex ecosystems by looking at vegetation cover and estimating how much carbon is stored in trees based on their maturity. Drones can rapidly plant trees over large areas and assess plants using laser technology known as Light Detection and Ranging (LiDAR). Meanwhile, autonomous underwater vehicles create 3D maps of underwater ecosystems, which, paired with artificial intelligence and machine learning, can identify at-risk coral ecosystems and track restoration progress.

Advances in AI also mean that researchers can do more with what they have to make better decisions and influence policy. It's far from a panacea, despite what those with skin in the game would have us believe, but a key enabler in overcoming barriers around scale, costs, and financing by simply figuring out what's what, faster. That information, however, is useless without action.

This is all with one big caveat: data collection is skewed towards the northern hemisphere, which already has a greater ability to build resilience and adapt to the climate crisis. Microsoft research found that there are five data scientists in the Global North for every one in the Global South.[59] When technology is built and programmed by a select few who all look, sound and think the same, the impact of that technology is limited and risks perpetuating existing injustices by overlooking people who are most at risk but have contributed the least to the climate crisis.

As the NASA time-lapse demonstrated, we are in this together and we are polluting the same atmosphere. Without a truly global perspective, we will miss something significant.

Blurring the lines

While tech-heavy and nature-focused approaches draw carbon out of the atmosphere and lock it away, some popular techniques blur the line between the two.

Scientists have long been interested in the dark soils found in some areas of the Amazon basin. In contrast to the area's regular, reddish lands, the dark soil now known as Terra Preta is uniquely fertile thanks to its high nutrients and carbon quantity. It originated in the Amazon basin at least 2,500 years ago, used by Indigenous peoples to boost crop productivity. Terra Preta inspired today's most popular form of carbon removal: biochar. Biochar is a carbon-rich material made by burning wood, manure or agricultural waste in an environment scarce of oxygen. This is just what ancient Amazonians did, slowly burning wood in soil pits with limited air.[60] The result can be mixed into soils, where it aids soil health and sequesters the carbon it contains; or it can be used as an additive in building materials like concrete and asphalt. Some claim that biochar makes concrete stronger and reduces its carbon intensity.[61]

Biochar is relatively low-tech and scalable, making it an attractive option for affordable CO_2 removal. Its permanence has been disputed, often ranging from 100-year mark[62] to thousands of years[63], depending on what it's made of. As such, biochar has dominated recent carbon removal sales.[64]

Proponents argue its versatility means it can be produced worldwide, offering a form of sustainable development when created and managed correctly.[65] For example, one company uses bamboo for biochar projects, providing locals with the tools, technology and training to produce and earn from it. One of its videos shows a thick bamboo forest in Prachinburi, Thailand, where offcuts are turned into biochar instead of burned.[66]

This adds to the circularity of bamboo farmers' operations as the biochar is spread back onto their land. In contrast to tech-heavy solutions, this encourages community involvement, which determines its success. Ensuring projects are correctly run with a community-first approach is key here, given there is also a risk of land-grabs.

Another low-tech approach is enhanced rock weathering (ERW), which accelerates a natural process in which certain rocks absorb CO_2 as they are exposed to air, water and soil. Rock dust is spread over large swathes of land, increasing the rock's surface area and allowing it to absorb more CO_2 as it weathers. The dust enriches soils as it releases nutrients like calcium, magnesium, and potassium, which can be a boon for farmers and improve crop yields.

One such company pursuing ERW is UNDO, which is positioning itself as the technology's "operating system", according to its founder Jim Mann.[67] It plans to scale up by providing underlying technology, science and routes to market so that anybody in the world can launch weathering projects.

However, both biochar and ERW are challenging to measure because they exist in open systems – it's hard to tell what's causing what and where the carbon ends up. In the case of ERW, the weathered minerals should form bicarbonates that eventually flow to the ocean in line with nature's carbon cycle. Proving the right reactions are happening, with carbon reaching a certain depth in the soil, is key to having certainty that it will happen. This is difficult, though, as even something as predictable as the season affects it.

Credits and controversy

Much of this technology is funded via carbon credits, which are tokens designed to represent one metric ton of CO_2 removed or prevented from entering the atmosphere. They have become such a pervasive way to offset emissions that you may have seen them on sale when you buy an airline ticket. They are bought and sold by various players, collectively dubbed the "voluntary carbon market" (VCM) because it's a non-compliance market, unlike Europe or California's cap-and-trade system, which covers only specific businesses and sectors.

Buyers opt for carbon credits when they want to offset their emissions, essentially paying someone else to remove or reduce CO_2 for them, with the money used to fund decarbonisation projects. Generally, the voluntary carbon market can be split into two categories: the first being so-called traditional "offsets" generated from avoided deforestation, tree-planting, cookstoves that are designed to release fewer pollutants; the second is removal credits, typically created by more novel technologies such as DAC, biochar and ERW. Mounting evidence suggests that traditional projects don't reflect genuine carbon savings, for example where deforestation threats were overstated or the baseline was inflated to increase the number of credits a project generates.[68] Removal credits, however, are distinctive by showing the actual removal of emissions rather than avoidance.

Many traditional offset projects also involve companies in the Global North paying those in the Global South to protect rainforest, mangroves or plant trees on their behalf. It's argued that this starves developing countries of their low-hanging fruit regarding decarbonisation; every country around the world must get to zero emissions but some may not be able to do so as cheaply as they would have been able to without selling carbon credits, raising concerns about neocolonialism and exploitation.

For Hans Westerhof, the co-founder and managing director of Remove, a CO_2 removal startup program, this isn't a large a concern.[69] The market is young, meaning there's enormous growth opportunity and developing countries are increasingly savvy on climate equity when it comes to the VCM. Indeed, Kenya, Ghana, the Bahamas and Mexico are just some countries that have explored the use of carbon credits to finance climate mitigation and adaptation.

Credits have also been used as a smoke screen, deterring meaningful climate action and allowing polluters to keep polluting. Critics see the VCM as a massive PR opportunity for companies being pressured to take climate action. There have certainly been flavours of this, but the public didn't take the bait. Many household names have faced backlash for their reliance on bad carbon credits, leading to greater due diligence, and policymakers cracking down on false claims.

Speaking to this is one study by non-profit Forest Trends, which claims companies that use carbon credits are decarbonising faster than those that don't.[70] Companies have tried to distance themselves from the VCM's earlier turbulence while a bevy of standard-setting organisations and guidelines have popped up in efforts to bring more credibility and transparency.

Carbon credits have varying price tags, with more permanent solutions raking in more per metric ton. The sought-after sweet spot is $100 per metric ton, which would make credits more affordable and help flush out cheaper, controversial offsets. This is still a bargain as the actual social cost of carbon is likely much higher when considering sick days and hospital visits intensified by the effects of the climate crisis.

While flawed, carbon credits do drive much-needed finance to nature protection, climate solutions and developing nations. The market doesn't dent the climate finance gap, which currently stands at $41 trillion for mitigation by 2030 and $600 billion for adaptation annually by 2050.[71] Still, it's a step in the right direction.

Prioritising people

Back in Newcastle upon Tyne, many miners were brought to their knees when former PM Margaret Thatcher closed the UK's deep coal mines in the aftermath of the historic 1980s strikes. Locals faced prolonged unemployment while the region slipped into economic decline. The scars of this can still be seen today, compounded by the loss of other heavy industries in the North East, like steel and shipbuilding. There were some retraining and support schemes for affected miners[72] but those lucky enough to find work often ended up in lower-paid jobs.[73]

Social inequality and the climate crisis are inherently linked. The green transition can be a force for good, if done right. As we shift away from fossil fuels, oil and gas workers face a similar rupture. A just transition is about uplifting currently overlooked communities and building the new economy inclusively. Still, it's also about ensuring jobs and reskilling programmes are in place for those who will lose out.

No matter the target, a people-first approach must be a priority. The US led the way with its Justice40 Initiative, which mandated that 40% of the overall benefits from investments in the Inflation Reduction Act and the Bipartisan Infrastructure Bill flow to disadvantaged communities. In early 2025, Trump's administration rescinded the initiative. Regardless of political status, companies building emerging climate technologies need a social licence to operate, so they should put communities first in a meaningful way, not just because it's required by law.

Chapter 2
Power

In a passionate 2008 speech, then-Vice President of the United States Al Gore challenged his country to produce 100% of its electricity from renewable and "truly clean carbon-free sources within 10 years". Gore likened this ambition to space travel. "Many people doubted we could accomplish that goal. But eight years and two months later, Neil Armstrong and Buzz Aldrin walked on the moon's surface," he told a crowd at D.A.R. Constitution Hall in Washington, DC.[74] Gore argued that the US could not withstand "10 more years of the status quo", of job losses and factory outsourcing, of sending billions every day for oil imports.

Those ten years have long passed. The US isn't powered by 100% renewable energy – just one-fifth of that number.[75] Globally, it's slightly less bleak at one-third.[76]

The current landscape

Not everyone has Gore's will. The technologies we need to eliminate fossil fuels from the energy grid have long existed, but we have failed to implement them with ambition. In fact, renewable energy growth has actually been underestimated throughout history. It's often boasted that we are on a better track than we thought as a result of this but energy still accounts for more than three-quarters of global emissions.[77]

Globally, the picture differs. Nearly 775 million people lived without any power in 2022[78] – never mind clean power. There is still a reliance on wood-burning stoves for cooking, which is bad for both the climate and health. These two problems are intrinsically linked, with the climate crisis exacerbating undernutrition, the spread of disease and heat stress.[79] A fossil-free world does not become a reality without the *whole* world transitioning – quickly. Every country has its own climate goals, but it bears repeating that pollution is a shared responsibility. The argument that developing countries should exploit fossil fuels for economic growth overlooks this. Many of these nations seek sustainable development, rather than following in the footsteps of the West's dirty dependency. It is a narrative critics believe is pushed by fossil fuel interests, as seen in a 2023 *Guardian* investigation that found Saudi Arabia attempted to create demand for oil and gas in developing countries.[80]

The path forward

Instead, investors are optimistic about "leapfrogging", where developing nations skip fossil fuels and head straight to renewables. There's evidence it's happening, as the Global South ramps up its renewables as the fastest way to industrialisation.[81] It's promising and logical. After all, many of these countries are also home to the materials needed for green energy infrastructure, which should buoy the industry, though this is typically exploited by the Global North, where both fossil fuels and colonialism are entrenched. Challenges around infrastructure and technology, skills and finance persist, depending on the country, but this is not dissimilar from developed countries, albeit to a different intensity. That's why projects like the Great Carbon Valley are so interesting, because it's trying to tackle a few of these problems at the same time.

Wind and solar have come on leaps and bounds in the Global North but there's still a considerable deployment gap for the scale and pace that's needed. Energy projects tend to struggle with permitting and workforce shortages while the materials required for infrastructure, including those troublesome batteries, come with their challenges. These are not new challenges and, instead of being seen as bottlenecks, should be considered a rallying call for the need for change.

In a net-zero future, our relationship with energy will be significantly different. Early adopters already use apps to monitor and manage energy use, but these platforms will be far more ubiquitous. Devices such as smart thermostats, EV chargers, and heat pumps will optimise energy use, aided by dynamic pricing with cheaper rates that encourages customers to put the washing on or charge their car outside of peak times. AI can help to automate this all, meaning energy could be something that we just passively consume. Today, these techniques also allow us to use power when it's green, though that shouldn't be a problem in a zero-emissions world.

But renewables don't generate energy around the clock, so making better batteries and energy storage systems are crucial. That's also where more stable power sources, such as nuclear, come into it. If limitless clean energy can be cracked, the potential benefits are enormous: dramatically reduced energy costs, the elimination of energy poverty and the creation of new industries that could drive innovation that were previously limited by energy intensity. DAC, for instance, would shake off some of its trouble.

Geopolitical tensions often stem from resource competition, namely fossil fuels. In an ideal world, a shift away from them could ease these. Right now, however, we see that you can't teach an old dog new tricks as Global North players plunder the Global South for its resources yet again[82]. Instead of this scramble, more effort must be made to open access to affordable green energy technologies, grid upgrade hacks and knowledge; without a global effort, we stand no chance of hitting zero emissions and zero fossil fuels.

Energy alchemy

The future energy mix will be diverse and dominated by renewables such as solar, wind, geothermal, hydropower and biomass, although the latter two pose social and environmental challenges. Nuclear, too, will play a small but essential role in balancing the grid, acting as baseload power, as it already does.

Hydropower, which generally uses water flow to generate electricity but comes in varying forms, was the largest form of renewable energy as of 2024.[83] Unfortunately, it has a history of harming nearby ecosystems and can displace local communities. For example, this construction of the WAC Bennett Dam in British Columbia, Canada, flooded 350,000 acres of forest and 175,000 hectares of villages, graveyards and cultural sites belonging to the Tsay Keh Dene Nation and other Indigenous communities. The energy generated by the dam didn't go to them either, instead making its way to more densely populated areas.[84]

Biomass is typically supported by investors, but it's not so clear-cut to me. Using land to grow crops for fuel instead of food is problematic when one in 11 people worldwide went hungry in 2023,[85] not to mention the fact that land is limited. While agricultural waste is commonly used as biomass, this relies on capturing the emissions, which, as we know, is not a sustainable solution. It is also not without its scandals. In 2024, power company Drax, which had clinched £6 billion in green subsidies in the UK at the time, was found to be burning old growth forest for energy.[86]

Wind and solar are already well established, vying for hydropower's crown as the most pervasive renewable energy. Once in place, they have no generation costs. However, this structure of energy grids skews pricing higher because energy costs are pegged to gas. More emphasis needs to be put on this – that cutting out fossil fuels benefits pockets as well as the planet.

Grid modernisation

In 1882, Thomas Edison flipped the switch on the world's first commercial and centralised power plant in New York City.[87] This marked the start of the electric age and laid the groundwork for Nikola Tesla's alternating current, which allowed energy to be transmitted over greater distances. Fast-forward to 1935 and the UK established the world's first integrated national grid. Since then, grids have been core to economic development and revolutionised many societies. Now, we look to renewables.

The intermittent nature of renewables means backup power sources must be available to ensure energy is available when people want it. Like power generation, storage will be a patchwork of different battery chemistries and technologies tailored. EVs themselves can be used as a distributed battery plant, banking energy at desirable times and feeding that back to homes or the grid later.[88] This concept alone adds incredible complexity to the current grid, which was built for constant and reliable fuel sources flowing just one way, though the situation is improving with new technology that can balance the grid more often.

Energy grids are an interconnected power generation and distribution network. Energy is generated, traditionally, by a coal-fired plant but increasingly by solar and wind, channelled through high- and low-voltage transmission lines all the way to local distribution networks that you see above your head in the street. From there, it's sent to our outlets, lights, EVs etc. Everything from software to sensors can be used to improve its management amid the increasing number of new, moving pieces. Together, this creates a "smart" grid as opposed to a "dumb" grid. Europe has the largest synchronous electrical grid globally, but even that needs to double in capacity to meet climate goals.[89]

The UK's National Grid has experimented with various grid-enhancing technologies to maximise the potential of existing infrastructure and ease congestion. Dynamic line rating is one such technology which monitors the real-time capacity of overhead power lines by crunching temperature, wind speed, and solar radiation data to optimise the energy flow and increase the power-carrying limit.

There are two schools of thought for necessary modernisation: distributed energy resources – like rooftop and balcony solar, electric vehicles as storage, and peer-to-peer energy sharing – or a continuation of the traditional centralised model we have today. Realistically, it will likely be a mixture of both.

Solar innovation

Today, solar panels are inefficient. They can convert around 20% of the energy that lands on them.[90] It may feel like solar is a done deal, but companies still have their heads down to improve how we harness the sun's radiation.[91] Innovation at the consumer level mainly comes down to business models and structure, which, as mentioned, has the potential to make energy more accessible. Distributed solar can enhance resilience, help balance demand, and promote social justice by allowing those without rooftops, such as renters or those who live in an apartment, to get involved with community and locally-owned projects. There's a growing interest in balcony solar amongst apartment-dwellers, where a couple of solar panels dangle from a balcony and can plug straight into the wall.[92] This breaks down some of the barriers to solar: no roof? No deep pockets? No worries.

There are plenty of off-grid opportunities too. While volunteering at an ecolodge on the outskirts of La Paz, Bolivia, I discovered solar ovens for the first time. The bright orange box on wheels, which had "I'm a solar oven :)" written on the back, was tucked away in the guest kitchen and stood out against gas ovens hooked up to mains. Versions of the same oven were given to Indigenous communities in the Bolivian Amazon to help them move away from toxic open-flame fires. Speaking with Shirley Pazos Bashualdo, Bolivian country director at Practical Action, the charity that ran the solar ovens projects, I learned that they also improved economic outcomes by allowing communities to dry seeds faster for jewellery production, then sold at local craft markets.[93] Alleviating financial pressure can only be good when such lands are at risk of being sold off to agriculture[94] or logging[95] encroachment. This is one example of how simple technologies can positively impact climate crises and livelihoods.

Community-first business

The co-operative business model is gaining traction, specifically applied to energy.[96] Whether it's Italy's ènostra[97] or The Amazonas Renewable Energy Cooperative, which runs projects in the Brazilian state of Amazonas, they are a way to connect local and sometimes rural communities to sustainable energy while giving them a say in how it's generated.[98] Instead of paying energy bills to a utility, members pay to maintain the systems they partially own, receiving energy in return. Some co-operatives serve as a purely financial investment, so the cash is seen as a payment for future cheap energy.

This set-up can increase energy efficiency, reliability, lower bills and generate local jobs which can be a boon for regional economies.[99] Empowering communities with their own energy production and consumption is only good considering mass centralisation has left many people in energy poverty. According to UK Government statistics, some 13% of households in England (3.17 million) were in fuel poverty in 2023.[100] I remember taking a metre key to the corner shop as a child and charging it with money before returning it to the "dumb" prepayment metre and loading up the funds. No money? No electricity. Sadly, many people still face this reality today.

At the same time, homes are increasingly equipped with electric stoves, heating, and better insulation.

While environmental upgrades are necessary for the environment, they can be exploited by property owners who jack up rent after installations to increase profits. This is known as green gentrification and can result in displacement if it's not carefully managed.

The key is to make it affordable. In places like Thailand, electrification programs have a tiered pricing structure that increases in parallel with energy use.[101] It's designed to discourage use and subsidise energy for those with less disposable income. It makes sense – the rich, who typically use a greater amount of energy, pay a little bit more so the poor can pay less.[102]

Microgrids, meanwhile, can play a central role in putting power back into the community's hands. They are set up by and serve small communities but are still connected to the larger network. While independent, if a line goes down, the outage can be contained, enhancing resilience and security. The catch is that they require a systematic rethink and evolution into a smart grid.

Large-scale solar and wind projects still have a role to play in providing reliable energy amidst local volatility. Wind projects, for example, can be spun up using the same co-operative structure but require vast swathes of land, which can be a constraint at the grassroot level. There's likely to be a bevy of third parties offering to manage and mediate such community-owned projects, with some, such as Ripple Energy, which earns money from setting up and managing solar park and wind farm co-ops already emerging.[103]

Corporations are also contributing through power purchase agreements (PPAs), which drive the development of wind and solar further by pre-agreeing to buy power from a new project. These could be co-located on site, on the roofs of huge warehouses or on land far away.

Energy projects, especially oil and gas, have a history of grabbing land without consulting local stewards, who are left to deal with the consequences. Today, projects are stalled when communities push back and often struggle to continue. If we want a seamless transition, it would make sense to work together from the get-go.

Transmission infrastructure

Investment in the global grid needs to double to more than $600 billion per year by 2030.[104] Some 80 million kilometres of power lines must be added or replaced by 2040 – the equivalent of the existing grid today – to achieve climate goals. The picture is mixed, even amongst rich countries: The Inflation Reduction Act (IRA) awarded $3 billion in loans and grants to support the buildout of transmission lines across the US,[105] though, again, at the time of writing, this is stuck in limbo under Trump's administration.[106] Meanwhile, Europe is set to invest over 1 billion euros ($1.1 billion) in cross-border infrastructure projects[107] and South Africa has earmarked $18 billion, but is struggling to raise the funds.[108]

As the distance between where energy is generated and consumed increases, miles of underground and overhead infrastructure are needed. Infrastructure upgrades must also prioritise sustainability by asking what materials are used. Where is the infrastructure located, and how does it affect disaster resilience? While many companies claim to expedite infrastructure development, few consider community needs. I have seen just one company that bucks that trend by using AI to design routes that account for environmental and social impacts, it claims.[109]

Proponents tout AI as a solution to many things but it's a catch 22. It sucks up valuable resources like energy and water and is why Sam Altman, the founder of OpenAI, the company behind generative chatbot Chat-GPT, is all-in on nuclear for its abundant energy. Data centres also require a lot of water for cooling, sometimes depleting nearby aquifers. In places where water is already scarce, this quickly becomes problematic.[110] No one should lose water thanks to our thirst for data.

Other tech companies are working in the physical world. UK-based company Asset Cool has designed coatings to improve transmission line capacity, and renewable energy provider Octopus Energy has invested in the Moroccan Xlinks project, which is an effort to connect Morocco and the UK via a 4,000km undersea cable and one of a handful in the race to spin up high-voltage lines.

Meanwhile, folks are working on improvements in turbine designs, solar panel efficiency and manufacturing processes to continue enhancing performance and reducing costs. If we can ace this, we will need less physical infrastructure and fewer materials to be mined, which cuts the carbon impact or producing green technologies, and we can get to zero emissions sooner.

Storing energy

Once energy is generated, it must be used or stored for later use. Due to a current lack of storage, we miss out on huge amounts of renewable energy every year, which would help balance daily and seasonal fluctuations in generation.

Lithium-ion (Li-ion) is the most dominant battery type today and earned its creators the Nobel Prize in Chemistry in 2019 due to its impact on the world.[111] Rechargeable batteries revolutionised wireless electronics and are crucial in making a fossil fuel-free world possible, as they are used for everything from mobile phones and laptops to electric cars and, increasingly, grid-scale energy storage.

Our reliance on this battery type is, however, concerning for society and the environment. One of the places lithium – known as "white gold" given the fervour that surrounds it – is extracted in South America via a water-intensive process in already dry areas, often to the detriment of locals.[112] The traditional process involves a series of evaporation pools, where water is evaporated leaving behind a brine full of different materials, including lithium. This is then refined, so the lithium is extracted. Cobalt, another essential component, is mined in the Congo, often by child exploitation.[113]

There are efforts to make this process less damaging, but the fact is that the characteristics of li-ion batteries don't make sense for large-scale battery plants that support the grid. Key amongst concerns is that they can be a fire hazard and are also difficult to recycle, creating toxic e-waste. This has sparked renewed interest in alternative chemistries with fewer risks.

Instead, lithium iron phosphate (LFP) batteries are gaining traction. The chemistry has a lower energy density than its popular cousin, meaning it can be used for fewer things, but it's free of nickel and cobalt, safer, and has a longer lifespan. Lithium iron phosphate dominates China's EV market, and carmakers BMW and Tesla are exploring its use.

Sodium-ion batteries also show promise and have the added advantage of using sodium, the world's sixth most abundant element, instead of lithium. Flow batteries, which use liquid electrolytes, can be scaled up easily and are also drawing attention. Both are considered safe and useful when high energy density isn't critical, like stationary grid storage. New chemistries could take some time to scale and commercialise, especially as they lack a supply chain on the scale of lithium-ion. Still, the push for sustainable battery materials is becoming a priority.

Some companies are working to produce lithium more sustainably through direct extraction. This process uses specialised membranes or chemical solvents to selectively capture lithium ions and leave other elements behind, reducing water use and environmental impact. It can also work with lower-grade lithium, opening up opportunities for extraction away from typical areas. For example, lithium has been successfully extracted from the north of England.[114] However, energy use and costs are still high, putting its feasibility into question.

Heat and electrification of transport

A considerable percentage of our energy is used for heat (50% of global energy use in 2018[115]) for industrial processes, to heat office blocks and homes. Heat energy storage, as a result, could revolutionise how we manage energy.

Heat today typically comes from fossil fuels and serves heavy industries like steelmaking, because it's quick and easy to fire up a furnace. Existing heat batteries don't get hot enough for this sector, but they show promise. For example, startup Rondo Energy claims to store and deliver high temperatures up to 1500°C for industrial applications in its thermal battery. They heat up the material and run ambient air past it when someone calls for heat, which is distributed as steam or water. Using inexpensive, off-the-shelf, abundant materials such as rocks, ceramics, salt and sand would also mean being able to slot into existing supply chains, aiding the scale-up journey.

What's particularly interesting about heat batteries is that they can be charged with waste heat from industrial processes or data centres. These are a darkening stain on our attempt to reach climate goals, given heavy industry is notoriously difficult to decarbonize and data centres are in increasing demand as a result of our AI appetite. Meanwhile, thermal solar can also harness the sun's heat to produce hot water or steam, but has struggled to gain momentum over the years. Naked Energy, a company that has bet on thermal solar since 2013, has multiple large-scale projects including atop the British Library in London.[116] "Money is going into moonshots and technology that might be available in 10, 15, 20 years time," CEO Christophe Williams told me, but "there are affordable technologies available today which need financing and political will."[117] His comments really get to the crux of this whole book.

As such, despite the potential, thermal solar and heat energy storage systems are often overlooked in some countries like the UK, where the focus has been primarily on heat pumps. They are common in countries near the equator, where sunny days are not few and far between. The innovations needed for a successful transition already exist and the challenge lies in business models along with political and social appetite, which varies globally. For instance, in the UK, it feels like EVs are a done deal. However, finding a viable business model for them is difficult in developing countries as many people lack the disposable income needed for private car ownership.

Instead of promoting individualism, investments should be made in public transport, which makes more financial and environmental sense. It has a lower per-person cost of travel, especially when the purchase price of vehicles, maintenance, insurance, and fuel are factored into it. It can also be electrified, generating much less emissions per mile while also reducing the overall number of vehicles on the road. Despite clear benefits to investing in public transport, the perceived lack of agency that comes with it makes it a difficult sell.

In regions where two-wheeled vehicles dominate, there's been significant work to convert these to electric. In just two years, EV company Spiro put more than 10,000 electric bikes on the road in four African countries.[118] Headquartered in the West African city of

Cotonou, Benin, it grew rapidly as riders were lured in with free motorbikes and the company earned money via a pay-to-use network of battery-swapping stations, where riders swap empty batteries for fully charged ones.

Geothermal is smoking

In the northern Atacama Desert of Chile lies the El Tatio geothermal field, the third-largest geyser site in the world. I arrived at 6am. The plumes of smoke, which can reach temperatures as high as 85°C, were vibrant and grand as the sun rose. The night and day mixing temperatures meant the geysers were in all their glory. This was another stop on my backpacking trip around Latin America.

Geothermal uses heat from the Earth's core to generate electricity or supply heat and these geysers are protected and not exploited, though abandoned equipment reveals echoes of a previous attempt to harness their energy. There are plenty like them around the world that were successfully exploited. That's how DAC company Climeworks powers its plants in Iceland, a country well known for its use of geothermal energy today, in sharp contrast to its historical reliance on oil and gas. Geothermal energy generates almost 25% of the country's electricity today.[119]

But it has roots elsewhere – in the now-UNESCO World Heritage Site of Pompeii, today known as an

Italian tourist hotspot after being frozen when nearby volcano Mount Vesuvius erupted in 79 CE. This city is believed to be one of the first places to harness geothermal energy to heat homes and use district heating to supply heat from a central source.[120] District heating is still used throughout Europe today, and is gaining traction elsewhere as an efficient method.[121]

Despite being tried and tested, investment in geothermal itself is patchy. Instead, investors are interested in technology that helps find new geothermal sites and systems that allow steam to be harnessed as energy. Enhanced geothermal systems (EGS) involve fracturing rock to create artificial reservoirs, potentially making geothermal viable in new locations. To me, the term "fracturing" i.e. fracking, echoes fossil fuel companies. However, startups are exploring these processes to increase efficiency and reduce environmental impact and costs. This does toe the line with fossil fuel expertise, meaning people affected by layoffs in traditional energy industries may find a home in geothermal operations.

Atomic energy

In the 1985 classic movie *Back to the Future*, the DeLorean time machine needs just 1.21 gigawatts of power – the equivalent of 10 million light bulbs – to operate, thanks to nuclear power. In the second movie, Doc

Brown has a "Mr. Fusion" home reactor that converts waste into energy.

This is quite literally science fiction but many are trying to make it a reality (nuclear fusion, not time travel. Though I'm sure people are working on that, too). Today's nuclear power comes from fission technology, splitting atoms to generate energy. In contrast, fusion creates energy by combining nuclei, the same process that naturally occurs in the sun.

Nuclear technology is controversial due to tragedies like the 1986 Chernobyl disaster when a RBMK reactor exploded, releasing huge amounts of radiation into the atmosphere, across a significant portion of Ukraine and beyond. However, nuclear power already plays a significant albeit limited role in the global energy system. Fission provides a reliable, low-carbon baseload electricity source but comes with high costs, long construction times, and public safety and waste management concerns. France is a frontrunner, relying on nuclear fission for up to 70% of its electricity.[122] In contrast, its neighbour Germany has shut all its reactors down.[123]

Companies like Oklo, backed by OpenAI founder Sam Altman, are developing smaller fission reactors to address some of these challenges. That includes "fast reactors" capable of recycling nuclear waste with just a smidge of fresh fuel, reducing waste toxicity and improving fuel efficiency. This reactor design was established back in

1951, but the cost has remained prohibitive. Russia is leading the use of these reactors, with many other countries exploring their viability.

There's a broader push to modularise fission in Small Modular Reactors, or SMRs. Like Oklo, proponents claim they will be safer than traditional nuclear systems due to their smaller size, passive safety measures, cooling, advanced materials and AI that allows for better modelling of reactor design. Advances in technology can't quell all safety concerns, though, especially when plants are placed in earthquake-prone areas like California.

The location of nuclear plants can raise issues of environmental injustice, as large power plants and waste facilities have historically been disproportionately placed in lower-income neighbourhoods. This exacerbates safety and even national security risks to specific groups, understanding infrastructure is often targeted in the event of conflict. There is also concern nuclear power could be propped up by subsidies that displace investments in solar and wind.

Cracking nuclear fusion is a dream for many. That's because it has the potential to generate abundant clean energy around the clock with minimal waste compared with today's reactors. That said, it's a well-known joke amongst energy experts that fusion has been just 20 years away for many decades.

It's polarising. You either love nuclear energy or hate it, but it's back in favour amongst tech circles due to the rising energy demands of AI. While alluring, nuclear energy at this scale remains hypothetical. Even if it is solved, it won't help us find an immediate solution today. It also doesn't promise energy equity, given that's a distribution problem rather than a technological one.

Other clean energy technologies, like improved solar, wind, geothermal, and energy efficiency measures are potentially faster to implement in the near term. Still, even for less controversial projects, public resistance, often characterised as "not in my backyard", and political foot-dragging hamper any meaningful development.

Clean energy without structural change could mean little for equity. As Sovacool puts it, "fusion could at least eliminate energy scarcity, but not energy poverty or insecurity."[124] The rationale? The world currently has enough surplus food, but we still have famine. While they were talking about fusion, this rings true for any clean energy project. How we distribute resources is a moral and political issue, and energy would be the same.

Chapter 3
Life from earth

Many people start their day with a cup of coffee. For me, it's a small ritual. I weigh out whole coffee beans, 12g per 200ml of water, and pour them into the grinder. They are ground to a fine powder, releasing a chocolate or citrus aroma (my favourite) and the kettle boils in parallel as I prepare the AeroPress. Today, my beans are from Colombia. It's been just a few months since I was in the South American country myself, roaming around coffee fincas, or farms, and their intertwined banana plantations.

It's difficult not to eagerly inspect the small Arabica trees when you see them in real life. Small clusters of red fruit hide amongst its evergreen leaves (often called a coffee cherry), the fruit being fundamental to modern life (at least to mine). From afar, I admired the countryside for its thick vegetation rather than the flat, treeless land waiting for me at home in England. I was staying on a finca in Manizales, deep in the country's coffee region, when a fellow traveller shattered my illusion. It's still agriculture, and it's still, mostly, monoculture, they pointed out.

Arabica, the world's most popular coffee bean, is at risk due to the changing climate. It's susceptible to temperature, meaning the warming planet reduces the number of areas it can grow. Unpredictable weather can also starve plants of what they need to thrive, while the previously-mentioned monocultures where just one crop or plant is grown at once are less resilient to pests and disease.

That stranger was right, to an extent. Banana trees and coffee plants are often "intercropped", which is a farming practice where two or more crops are grown alongside one another, each for increased resilience and decreased biodiversity harms, which is a significant improvement on monocultures.[125] As such, it is a key strategy in biodiversity conservation. Banana trees shade coffee trees and can stay hydrated during extreme heat, meaning the coffee tree doesn't need to compete with it for water, which adds to the crop's resilience.

This relationship demonstrates the intricate interconnectedness of plant species; just as humans rely on each other to survive, plants do too. It's not just what you can see: all the layers at the ground level and below create a complex web of species and layers that support a resilient and efficient ecosystem. From the tiniest bacteria found in arctic ice to the foxes that roam London's streets, that's biodiversity.

The importance of biodiversity

Biodiversity underpins the worldwide economy. For instance, pollination provides food – a mighty task taken up by the world's insects; water is filtered by trickling through a complex underground network of roots; some go deep, others go wide, each acting as a sieve and purifying water. Air is generally purified through photosynthesis as trees and plants can capture pollutants in their leaves' tiny hairs. When this pollution falls to the ground, some soil bacteria can break it down.

These may seem like simple functions, but they all feed into capture of CO_2, mitigating heating effects in dense areas and supporting overall food security, until overconsumption tips the scales.

Coca-Cola, for example, uses nearly two litres of water for each litre of its beverages.[126] Alternatively, imagine how different modern medicine would be if we hadn't formulated Aspirin, which comes from the bark of a willow tree, which has long been used to treat pain by ancient civilisations. More than half of the world's GDP, $44 trillion, comes from nature and its "services".[127] In humanity's pillaging of the natural world, we've subsequently thrown it out of balance. Indeed, according to a 1968 speech by President Robert F Kennedy, GDP "measures everything in short, except that which makes life worthwhile".[128]

Humanity has steadily encroached on natural habitats for centuries, replacing thriving ecosystems with high-rises and concrete to make way for our gas-guzzling cars and consumerism. During the COVID-19 pandemic, we witnessed a powerful demonstration of human influence on the world when ecosystems received a rare chance to recover in our absence. Stories of resilience and regeneration appeared; the Italian city of Venice, otherwise littered with tourists and cruise ships, saw dolphins return to its canals;[129] Cape Town saw penguins roam its streets;[130] and, for Wales, it was goats that ran "riot".[131] Earth itself physically calmed during this period also as seismologists reported lower vibrations from human activity than before the pandemic.[132]

However, despite this break, criminal land-grabbing, deforestation, mining and poaching increased during the pandemic while conservation efforts paused,[133] exemplifying humanity's incessant need for control over natural resources. After centuries of habitat destruction, pollution, and overexploitation, biodiversity is facing a crisis parallel to climate change. Addressing this is an urgent and vital part of the puzzle if we want to restore environmental balance.

Its current state

Biodiversity conservation has deep roots in public consciousness. Yellowstone, which sprawls 2.2 million acres in the US, became the first national park in 1872 after expeditions documented the area's distinctive geothermal, wildlife and natural beauty. These discoveries led to public pressure from scientists and artists to preserve the area and its natural inhabitants for future generations. With Earth losing species at unprecedented rates, mainly due to human activity, scientists are still discovering thousands of new species yearly, revealing how much of the world remains uncharted.[134]

Today, we're at a critical crossroads where some businesses and governments increasingly recognise their dependence on healthy ecosystems. This was not the case just a few years ago, when businesses treated nature as a nice-to-have. The reality is, however, productivity relies on natural systems. This is still not widespread and the disconnect reveals a fundamental flaw in today's business models and is a narrative that needs to change – we must move from deeming nature as a luxury to considering it as the foundation of functioning economic systems.

Policymakers have begun responding to this after years of advocacy, just like Yellowstone, culminating in groundbreaking new legislation in the EU and UK, which will have a cascading impact beyond their borders.

The Corporate Sustainability Due Diligence Directive (CSDD) will require big businesses to ensure that their products don't harm people and the environment by addressing their supply chains' social and environmental impacts.[135] The complementary and ambitious Nature Restoration Law requires all EU countries to develop detailed action plans to restore habitats and enhance nature.[136] These plans should cover at least 20% of the EU's land and sea areas by 2030 (the equivalent size of France and Portugal together) with work on all degraded ecosystems in progress by 2050.

These European projects feed into a broader effort to address deforestation in supply chains, which will inadvertently protect biodiversity and implement the landmark Global Biodiversity Framework. The framework, touted as biodiversity's answer to the Paris Agreement, aims to protect 30% of all lands and oceans by 2030, halt and reverse degradation and funnel $700 billion in annual investment into the space by 2030.[137]

This funding target, identified in 2019 research by the Nature Conservancy as the gap for beating biodiversity and nature loss, is an enormous and intangible financial commitment.[138] However, even a figure *that* big is relative to the value of a functioning society, human health and survival. Degraded ecosystems erode mental health and threaten the livelihoods of millions worldwide who rely on nature and natural resources, but people don't typically price in environmental destruction. Biodiversity and the natural world are also central to identity, traditions, and spirituality, which should make the cultural case for protecting them.

Ultimately, this should be less of an economic question and more about safeguarding humanity and society. Still, given the system we operate within, someone must make the financial case.

Technology as an enabler

There are many technologies that need both the social and financial case to stand, which we'll look at here. Remote monitoring systems, sensors and data analytics are now complimented by AI's ability to crunch and make sense of vast datasets and have been popular amongst investors. This is thanks in part due to lessons learned in the VCM, with companies seeking to avoid the greenwashing scandals that plagued carbon credits.

Still, even the most sophisticated systems aren't a silver bullet. Technology enhances capabilities needed to solve the climate and nature crises, but its effectiveness relies on clear regulatory standards, verification processes and meaningful accountability. Such a network of co-dependencies is broadly referred to as 'measurement, reporting and verification' (MRV) or geospatial infrastructure, which spans the gamut: satellites, lasers that scan and map the earth, an array of sensors, camera traps and microphones hidden in forests.

Gaps do emerge despite the various forms of technologies that collect data, so the question is, what can be done to fill in missing information? There's no easy answer. Rather, we just have to do it all, at least do what makes sense to ensure the most holistic coverage we can. Here's a whistle-stop tour of the technology being used today.

Satellites

Remote sensing via satellites is well established and increasingly sophisticated; scientists now have a much better understanding of the planet's overall health and specific ecosystems than blunt data on how much forest has been lost.

The first satellite launched to observe our fragile planet was the Soviet Union's Sputnik 1. Now, there are more than 10,000 in low Earth orbit.[139] Many of them are owned by Elon Musk's Starlink, which are primarily designed to provide internet, but others are specifically for tracking and understanding our changing planet.[140]

Improving how well satellites can see, their resolution, has been revolutionary. Some systems are now capable of snapping pixel-level information when looking at a specific area of Earth. Using this data and a calculation of near-infrared light, from either satellites or aerial surveys, the Normalized Difference Vegetation Index (NDVI) metric can figure out the state of vegetation and its density as well as different land types like sand and soil. This information is all essential for biodiversity assessments and urban planning. New lasers can even penetrate water to varying depths, which could help us to better understand coral reef bleaching and sea temperatures.

LiDAR

Light Detection and Ranging (or LiDAR) compliments satellite monitoring by shooting a laser beam from a plane or drone to create detailed 3D mapping of landscapes, vegetation and other structures.

By scanning pockets of Earth with millions of light points, LiDAR unlocks large-scale measurement of land, providing data on the structure of habitats and the condition of ecosystems. Habitat structure is a key part of measuring ecosystem condition as it allows for a three-dimensional view that can reveal the composition of species, the structure of the habitats that they live in, and how the ecosystem functions as a whole.

Despite hopeful use cases and its effectiveness, LiDAR's use is currently limited – but that is beginning to change. Even the most promising tech has a kryptonite: simple cloud coverage, which blocks signals sent down to Earth, creating data gaps.

Environmental DNA

Environmental DNA analysis, or eDNA, is an emerging technique used to establish what genetic material is present in water or soil samples, implying what species are in the ecosystem. Proponents argue it can capture a broad spectrum of species without disturbing them in their natural habitat, while also spotting invasive species early. eDNA is also cheaper and quicker than traditional surveys, especially in challenging or remote environments.

Despite its advantages, eDNA's reliability is questioned because it detects genetic material rather than organisms. When fish DNA is found in a river sample, for example, it's not known whether the fish was alive and present in that specific location the day the DNA was collected – or whether it was pooped out by another animal, or washed downstream.

It also doesn't indicate species abundance, crucial for conservation efforts and understanding ecosystem health, as it indicates how species populations are changing – are they stable, growing or declining in this ecosystem? eDNA is just one tool in our arsenal for beating the climate and biodiversity crises and must be used alongside others.

Listening to nature

There's no mistaking the hum of a cricket in the countryside, but how many other species can you hear over that distinctive noise? Bioacoustics is dedicated to recording nature's sounds to monitor and study biodiversity. When paired with audio libraries, sound sensors can reveal animals' presence. This approach is particularly valuable for tracking nocturnal or quiet species, and for large-scale, long-term monitoring, including in remote areas.

While bioacoustics can be as simple as stashing a microphone in the forest, newer tools can be connected via Bluetooth and send real-time alerts to researchers. This also proves useful for detecting invasive species, illegal deforestation and poaching activities. Recordings tell you what's making noise but not, crucially, why, which is a major constraint.

Camera traps

Camera traps (hidden cameras, essentially) offer similar benefits, visually. Imagine a GoPro fixed to a metal rod, concealed in a river. Researchers use bait to attract fish and other marine life, which would approach the camera, giving researchers valuable footage of species up close in their natural environment.

Larger animals like mammals are easily documented with camera traps, while birds are more difficult to spot. The latter can instead be identified through their song via acoustic sensors, making the case for a patchwork of monitoring technology.

Together, bioacoustics and camera traps have revolutionised wildlife research, conservation, and storytelling as visual and audio have a rare ability to capture the public imagination. Consider David Attenborough's documentaries – his production team has documented rare and elusive animals over long durations due to technology like this.

The relative simplicity and accessibility of hidden cameras or microphones also democratise wildlife monitoring for land stewards or curious individuals with little understanding of the environment. One researcher told me that Indigenous people in the Amazon rainforest are using camera traps, drones and satellite phones during territorial patrols to protect their land.

Artificial intelligence

Aside from the funding challenges, protecting and restoring nature often comes down to data availability: researchers need to understand what exists in ecosystems, what's changing and what to do about it. These datasets have traditionally been too large and complex to be processed by humans in a time and cost-effective way, but AI and machine learning cracked open the ability to analyse, monitor and predict changes over time.

How AI is developed and scaled already feels out of our hands, controlled by a select few who have concentrated power in the space, but independent researchers are pushing for human oversight for an essential counterbalance, and even quality control, of the technology.

AI is both a solution and a contributor to the climate crisis. Proponents argue it will help us save the planet, solve global health issues, and reshape society to be more fair, but its guzzling of natural resources is doing harm today, intensifying these issues. To develop huge, generalist systems such as Chat-GPT, which is built on a large language model, we're being asked to accept an unknown and potentially endless cost that could never pay off. More focused systems, known as small language models, are an alternative path forward as their size means a lower energy, compute and cost demand.[141] They have a specific dataset and therefore a case for usage, say for water or biodiversity, and would allow us to reap the rewards of AI while doing less damage.

Turning data into action

I've written extensively on how the climate and nature crises threaten businesses, infrastructure, and communities. The technology discussed tracks and analyses ecosystems, designed to plug gaps in data on the natural world and aid decision-making. It's this data that's used by technology companies trying to predict when extreme heat, flooding and droughts will occur so that we're better prepared when they do. It is only meaningful when it informs specific, measurable action plans.

Perhaps one of the most difficult places to track is the vast, open ocean. Take coral reefs: they are the beating heart of marine ecosystems and economies but face creeping threats. Despite efforts from the likes of Global Coral Reef Monitoring Network, which, as the name suggests, operates worldwide, the reality is that monitoring is limited.

Increasing temperatures and ocean "heat waves" pose the greatest risk,[142] causing coral bleaching which ultimately kills coral if it has no time to repair between bleaching events. Targeted restoration can get started once high-risk reefs are identified, which is often done through high-powered satellites, or remotely operated vehicles that scan the seafloor.

Some researchers are 3D printing artificial reefs that mimic actual reefs based on data collected from existing ecosystems.[143] While artificial reefs face a myriad of challenges that throw their usefulness into question, 3D printing can provide customised tools that better integrate the physical and fundamental details of natural reefs, such as their texture and complexity. Following that, eDNA and 3D imaging can be used to assess the reef's effectiveness, demonstrating real-world applications of these technologies.

Researchers will always have a wish list of wants and needs – like audio devices with longer batteries and faster feedback loops on machine learning – but these improvements will come as they, private companies and investors continue to drive innovation and adoption. We're fortunate to live at a time where technologies, many of which have existed for decades in the pages of science fiction books, now exist to solve many of our crises; the challenge is ensuring they scale fast and cheaply enough to increase adoption. Part of the solution will be cultural, to move away from valuing nature only when it's threatened, and to find unlikely collaborators.

The climate crisis is inherently intersectional, meaning solutions should be too. Organisations, researchers, companies and communities must work together but this isn't how it happens in practice. Researchers must compete with each other, vying for the same pool of grant funding on a project-by-project basis; early-stage companies get bogged down with the long sales cycles of incumbent industry players; and larger companies are bound by returning cash to investors or shareholders rather than outcomes for the planet.

There are pockets of intersectionality to take inspiration from. In 2023, I was fortunate enough to interview two scientists applying bone research to better understand the fragility of coral reefs. It highlights an unlikely cross-pollination of ideas that stemmed from curiosity and a coffee at Heriot-Watt University in Scotland, where they both worked at the time of their meeting. The similarities between porosity in corals and osteoporosis are "mind-boggling", material scientist Uwe Wolfram, who focuses on bones and was working on the project with marine biologist Sebastian Hennige, told me at the time.[144]

I don't doubt that tech and humanity coexist harmoniously, with the former enabling the latter to live happily. From an equity perspective, anyone implementing projects, with or without technology, must have free prior and informed consent and proper benefit-sharing agreements with local or affected communities. With that, tech can be a powerful ally in conservation efforts. The key to scaling up these technologies is their intersection with existing and ancient knowledge and community engagement, which could usher in a new era of conservation.

It also challenges our perception of data sources, a conversation which modern science has dominated thus far. Where has that gotten us when it comes to climate action, Cambridge climate change scholar Professor Mike Hulme probed at an "Epistemic Pluralism and

Climate Change" talk hosted at the London School of Economics that I attended in early 2025.[145] He was making the case for interdisciplinary perspectives and a greater inclusion understanding passed through generations via oral histories, folklore and stories, informal knowledge systems and practical adaptation strategies developed by communities.

When I interviewed environmental and Indigenous rights advocate and attorney Tara Houska for an article in 2023,[146] she explained how this is part of her work.[147] The concentration of biodiversity on lands stewarded by Indigenous peoples is not an accident, she confirmed.[148] Rather, it's due to their relationship with nature and an understanding that we are not in dominion of it.

In all, think of it as active stewardship but empowered by technology – as it always should have been.

Chapter 4
Imagining the future

When I asked the 30 or so activists, scientists, innovators and investors I spoke with for this book what their ideal, sustainable future looked like, they often replied with imagery of renewables where everyone has access to clean energy, food, and a home at a price point that's affordable for them. They envisioned focusing on resilient, localised systems and regenerative practices, where public financing, business engagement, and traditional conservation actions are in place to fund climate and nature protection and restoration. Such a shift would also change the shape of supply chains, seeing a rise to smaller and local infrastructure, including energy production via microgrids.

Some go further. In this future, the material world borrows heavily from nature. Just look at Velcro – Swiss engineer George de Mestral invented the sticky mechanism after being inspired by the way burdock burrs stuck to his dog's fur.[149] On the other hand, some wind turbine designs borrow from humpback whale fins, which have great aerodynamics.[150]

Our world doesn't fully take advantage of these possibilities. The notion of solving the climate crisis with a deterministic outlook of "technology will save us all" is frequently questioned, understandably so. It's undoubtedly ironic to rely on technology as the solution considering it got us here in the first place, but delayed action has forced our hands and we don't have time to waste.

We have known about the dangers of climate change for more than 40 years, and many have shouted from the rooftops over that time, with limited success. Having worked their fingers to the bone, some researchers now believe this is the maximum that was achievable in the last 40 years. But this has been woefully inadequate. Society members, businesspeople, policymakers and students have a responsibility and a role to play in achieving a sustainable future. Our voices must be heard.

The false dichotomy

The first thing we must do is challenge the sweeping generalisation that protecting the environment hinders growth – this is not true. It is a reductive party line for politicians and business people to maintain the status quo. Economic growth and personal freedoms do not need to conflict with environmental protection. The two are of course inextricably linked, and now, more than ever, society is waking up to the fact that protecting the Earth and its systems shouldn't be out of the goodness of their heart but because it makes economic sense.

2025 research by Boston Consulting Group found that up to 34% of global GDP is at risk without significant climate action, translating to the global average temperature rising to 3°C by 2100.[151] That's above the current trajectory for the same timeframe, according to Climate Action Tracker, which, as of November 2024, estimates warming of 2.6°C based on current 2030 targets.[152] This heat will be insufferable for many people worldwide, and already is. For example, the UK's sweltering 40-degree heat in July 2022 was just a fraction of what's felt elsewhere in the world. These numbers are an urgent call to action.

Next, we need to ditch GDP as a measurement of success. To its credit, GDP served a purpose during World War II when measuring the total value of goods and services, which was critical for war planning. That cemented it as an economic measure, but even its inventor, Simon Kuznets, who came up with the concept during the great depression, warned against using it as a sole measure of progress, as it didn't account for wellbeing.[153]

War and natural disasters can boost productivity after an initial dip due to reconstruction and investment and, quite clearly, that shouldn't count as simple progress. It's worth remembering that our perception of progress and which technologies have played a role in it or have been made viable is due to specific actors and stakeholders who look at narrow metrics, many of whom also have skin in the game.

Community collaboration

To look outward from these self-interested stakeholders, community engagement approaches should be found so that the community and policymakers can meet in the middle, from both top-down and bottom-up methods. Many scholars say that solutions to the climate crisis need to start with the community. We also need to see social entrepreneurship, social changes, how we manage our societies, and how wealth is distributed within and between countries so that it's not concentrated in developed nations or by companies from such nations.

A fundamental problem is that these communities, and the international bodies and governments that have the funding and power, rarely meet in the same room; they attend different events. There is the yearly Conference of the Parties, but this hierarchical structure perpetuates existing power structures. The development of solutions could move faster if it were more of a network with equal footing for local community leaders.

The pace is essential: international efforts take too long, but taking action on climate doesn't have to be hard or indecipherable; it can be as simple as communication tools. Technology could debug jargon terminology that excludes non-specialists, supporting existing attempts to get everyone around the same table. The IPCC, for example, has attempted to be more inclusive of Indigenous knowledge, but representation remains a challenge.[154] The UNFCCC is trying to do the same with the Santiago Network, which attempts to close the technical knowledge gap in developing countries particularly exposed to the climate crisis.[155]

The types of technologies used, and where and how, should be tailored to each place, still poses challenges of scale – whether something will take off depends on the country, community needs, and context. Ultimately, a community needs assessments and benefits agreements should precede any action. The organisation implementing technology should also be continuously held accountable throughout the process.

Policy as a lever

China is often dubbed the first "electrostate" due to its rapid uptake of renewable electricity and manufacturing of solar, EVs and batteries.[156] It also relies heavily on nuclear power. Globally, the superpower leads the way in energy adoption. Much of this comes from ambitious government policies and subsidies that nurture the industries. Denmark, too, has been a pioneer in wind energy[157] thanks to grassroots experimentation, innovation and friendly policy.[158]

It speaks to how governments play a crucial role in making sustainable options economically viable, be it through ramping up manufacturing of climate tech on home turf or incentivising faster deployment. The UK and Europe, however, have primarily focused on research and development of new technologies, meaning there are plenty of compelling plays, but not many can scale to the point that is needed.

Why is that? It comes down to politics; in some countries, there is pushback against increased government spending and interventions. This is particularly sticky when populations live below the poverty line. How can we fund tech that may ultimately fail when so much else is at risk? But the majority of technology today has likely received some sort of research and development support to grow from a seedling into a sapling and onwards.

On the other side of the political spectrum, others believe that the free market should be allowed to run rampant and that businesses without sound economics should fail. Realistically, the free market doesn't exist, as the government has always been a guiding hand.

There's pressure from elsewhere, too: the fossil fuel industry. The sector and its propaganda machine is pervasive. They have infiltrated think tanks, trade bodies, and politics to lobby governments, successfully obstructing or watering down policies that go against the gas-guzzling narrative they've perpetuated for so long. Climate solutions subsidies have to come from somewhere – perhaps fossil fuel companies are worried it will be from their $7 trillion pot.[159]

Adopting clean energy and electrification could have happened much quicker without these dynamics. Some of today's technologies that are unproven at scale could have already gone mainstream, while carbon pricing would likely be compulsory, widespread, and more expensive. Policy naturally does change depending on governments in power, so instruments targeting the climate crisis would likely be more consistent, as there wouldn't be so much short-termism.

Subsidies are one tactic that fits within existing systems, but as discussed earlier, we can't just grow our way out of this problem. New strategies are needed – and fast. We have to challenge this system.

Norway's Government Pension Fund, which Norges Bank Investment Management runs, was established in 1990 after Norway discovered oil in the North Sea in

1969, initially set up as a buffer against oil revenue volatility. It serves as both a financial reserve and a long-term savings plan, "so that both current and future generations of Norway benefit from our oil wealth."[160]

For its time, this was forward-thinking. It's largely considered a successful project because it helps fund Norway's welfare state without raising taxes to unsustainable levels and provides many other social benefits. Of course, wealth inequality still exists. Unlike other petrostates, Norway worked hard to diversify its income thanks to the fund, worth $1.8 trillion as of January 2025,[161] providing stability. Today, there is a massive market for renewables and EVs, and it holds the title for the highest EV adoption rate globally. Nearly all of Norway's electricity comes from renewable sources, primarily hydropower,[162] although it also greatly benefits from oil export profits.[163]

Norway also avoided the "resource curse", when countries rich in natural resources struggle with slower economic growth and development. My assumption is that it's because Norway is close to Europe and not colonised by its neighbours, unlike much of the rest of the world that sat and continues to sit on top of precious resources and often cheap labour.

So, what would happen if each country had set up a fund like this and given back to its people and those it exploited? The trajectory of many still-developing nations could have been entirely different. Reinvesting a share of the profits – gained from extracting the wealth of others in the first place – into health, education, and public infrastructure would have helped to bridge development gaps, reduce global inequality, and shift power dynamics by giving exploited nations greater bargaining power. As countries would receive a share of the profits, it would be an all-around more ethical way to extract resources.

Governments and companies developing global technologies should let this marinate. Sure, colonial powers at the time would likely not have done this willingly, but would they now? Supply chains are increasingly global. This poses the question: could a modern version of a compulsory investment fund be used as a blueprint for reparations today?

Some businesses have been working with communities affected by their projects, say local solar farms, through community benefit agreements (CBAs) which emerged in the early 2000s.[164] Early versions were criticised as a way for extractive industries to exploit local communities without delivering on benefits, even though they were used as a tool for community-buy-in or a social licence to operate. Today, the concept has a lot of currency. However, it's worth noting that a significant power imbalance still exists in initial negotiations.[165]

To access US federal funding introduced by President Biden, particularly the Bipartisan Infrastructure Law and the Inflation Reduction Act, applicants were required to include a CBA with provisions for local job creation, profit-sharing, infrastructure development or other community investments. This is tied to the broader Justice40 initiative, which Trump rescinded,[166] but it shows countries how community-first approaches could work.

While this work attempts to give affected and disadvantaged communities a slice of the pie, many other policy levers can be pulled in parallel to force or incentivise polluters to act. For example, civil and environmental engineer Delton Chen has developed the Global Carbon Reward, a proposed playbook for managing climate risk.[167] He suggests various strategies to decarbonise the economy via a new carrot-and-stick method.

First, a carbon reward – it's specifically *not* a tax, Chen told me[168] – backed by central banks would have a rising price floor, gradually pushing the reward for mitigating pollution. It would complement Europe's cap and trade system, a compulsory carbon market, where polluters are given emissions certificates – which serve as the "cap" every year – and have to buy more from less-polluting companies if they go over their budget. The cap is gradually decreased.

The mechanism would work alongside other incentives but wouldn't just benefit big companies. Chen argues for decentralised financial rewards for qualifying communities and individuals who reduce emissions or remove them from the atmosphere, where practical. This is entirely different to how the market currently looks, with individuals excluded from benefiting for their actions (not that the responsibility should fall on their shoulders).

One sticking point is the price tag: how do we find a market price that's higher than the value of forest products, which often come with deforestation or wider destruction. Many of the technologies we need to transition to a more sustainable world need resources from everywhere; their development needs to be supported by a willingness to share our resources while also reducing overconsumption. Perhaps, also, a greater understanding of how halving your living space and taking the bus affects people and the planet – locally and globally.

Traditional economics focuses primarily on allocating money and resources rather than distribution, as one of the first ecological economists, Herman Daly, points out.[169] Chen's work, however, brings about many justice opportunities. Land stewardship is often unrewarded in existing markets but, if implemented, the Global Carbon Reward could channel cash to those who need it to protect our more precious ecosystems for generations.

Pushing back on growth

Ecological economists, such as Daly, argue that reshaping the economy generally requires achieving three different goals, thus requiring three different policy mechanisms. The cap-auction-trade system is evidence of this.

"First, a quantitative limit is set, reflecting judgments of sustainable scale. That is, a previously unlimited or free good is recognised as scarce, and the scale of its use is quantitatively limited. Second, the newly scarce good or right is now a valuable asset – who owns it? Deciding who owns it is a question of distributive justice. Third, once scale and distribution decisions have been collectively decided, we can have individualistic market trading and efficient allocation, at least for most rival and excludable resources," he told economics professor Jamie Morgan in 2019.[170]

But limits are crucial, they say: the limiting factor of growth is increasingly the natural world, not artificial capital or money. Many call for intersectional approaches that consider social identities, recognise how different forms of oppression and power imbalances intersect with environmental issues, and ensure that policies address these systemic social injustices.

Economist E. F. Schumacher was sceptical of pure market plays. He didn't address climate finance but advocated for decentralisation, sustainability, and human-centric approaches. There are some efforts to do this, such as in the Peruvian Amazon where a basic income pilot program aimed to pay an Indigenous community for their work looking after the land,[171] but it was never explicitly said that is what cash would be used for. The founder of the charity Cool Earth, Matthew Owen, told me it showed promising initial results, including improved nutrition and reduced poverty among participating households.[172] It is just one example of how social causes can be furthered by incentives to look after the climate or vice versa.

The B Corp Aidkit, which is partnering with Cool Earth to provide payment infrastructure technology for the project, was initially set up during the pandemic to help distribute funds to undocumented workers excluded from government assistance programs.[173] It still works with governments, NGOs, and community groups to help distribute cash to those most in need, with a focus on disaster relief, showing how it will play a crucial role in distributing support in the future.

While this doesn't directly reduce emissions, it's a great example of facilitator technology. For those that do, however, new mechanisms like the Global Carbon Reward could see them rewarded. A systemic approach could also see climate action turned into an investable asset to then be used as a hedge against climate risks.

We need to rethink how we fund society in the aftermath of a disaster and climate tech funding models as current technologies rely heavily on volatile private market appetite. Investors have helped to create some climate tech segments but are also driven by profit, which creates a conflict of interest. Other types of capital and financing models are needed to scale climate tech, especially for early-stage companies and those in developing countries.

Nonprofits and foundations focused on conservation can provide funding for mapping and protecting biodiversity, but are often risk-averse. They can also collaborate with partners to provide climate and biodiversity research resources. However, they are often bound by their funders and usually can't speak out when they breach climate goals.

Meanwhile, big corporations and businesses that rely on natural resources should invest in climate change solutions, biodiversity protection, and restoration to offset their impacts. This could be tied into water accounting and tracking other resource use.

We've talked a lot about economics and policy, but could the answer be something as simple as art? Communicating climate solutions clearly is fundamental and artistic entertainment shouldn't be dismissed. For example, the founder of Arts and Climate Change and artist Nicole Kelner started on her path of climate communication by making 100 days of flashcards, diving into a new topic daily, learning as much as possible, and distilling it into a visual.[174] That was her way of learning, soaking up all this information and then presenting it to the world, hoping that others would learn that way too.

Ultimately, to achieve arcadia, we need a lot of money and a stronger emphasis on people, not profit. At face value, that may seem contradictory, but it just lacks creativity.

Conclusion
Completing the climate puzzle

I write this in spring. Cherry blossoms have bloomed, lining the North London streets where I now live with endless shades of pink. Petals fall onto the concrete road, trampled on by school children and commuters like myself, out of breath from the rat race day in and day out. It's easy to get swept away by life, concerned only with the day-to-day and disengaged with humanity's broader impact on society. It's just as easy to feel hopeless, like we have made little progress on the climate and nature crises. They are, after all, vast and nuanced problems.

It's true; we are still not on the right trajectory. We keep emitting, so we haven't even bent the curve yet, which is devastating. What we need to achieve by the day is getting steeper and steeper, though some expect peak emissions to be hit soon. The urgency of the climate crisis is pressing, and we must act now, as every moment counts.

Through the book, I hope to have shown you that nature-based solutions, green infrastructure, and technology can offer a path forward when designed inclusively. We just need the political and financial will to put them into action quickly.

Solutions span the gamut; from farming and land use to sucking CO_2 directly out of the atmosphere and recycling materials to figuring out new battery chemistries. The task at hand looks enormous. However, this also means the potential for action is significant. The diversity of solutions available should inspire hope and motivate us to act, as each option, no matter how small, contributes to the larger cause.

We have discussed how finance restricts this type of climate action. As these challenges are overcome and solutions are scaled up, governance structures must be in place to lure investors in and keep them mission-aligned. Community benefit agreements must ensure equitable benefit sharing, grievance mechanisms and community consent when implementing biodiversity credit projects.

Remember that we need a systems-wide rethink. We won't achieve any progress if we continue with the mindset of Western powers doing what they want and failing to consider Indigenous knowledge, land ownership, and biodiversity services. There's a real opportunity here to build alongside often underrepresented communities.

This holistic approach should look beyond just measurement to address systemic gaps in data, knowledge, governance and financing models while focusing on equity, biodiversity and climate justice. It includes coming up with a new way to define success, as measuring progress via GDP simply doesn't work in a world that should prioritise healthy ecosystems. This is where we start to realise that it's not about the lack of or the existence or viability of many technological solutions, it's about neoliberal capitalism and putting profit ahead of everything else. We're on a finite planet with finite resources and can't just have exponential growth.

After all, the climate crisis is just a symptom of capitalism and colonialism, which incentivise injustice. These systems are all too effective in achieving the results they are set up to achieve – wealth and power. We must address this underlying issue. At an individualistic level, the most significant lever somebody could pull is helping to empower others to learn, realise, understand or find their way to keep having hope.

The message is clear: the time for effective action regarding climate and nature is now. The window is rapidly closing, demanding immediate and decisive steps to protect biodiversity and mitigate the effects of the climate crisis. We must decarbonise rapidly while maintaining 92 biodiversity and natural carbon sinks; we should prioritise nature and embrace technologies that help us do so, given that healthy ecosystems are our best defence against climate change.

The climate crisis is not a one-size-fits-all problem, nor should the solutions be. We must understand that climate solutions can't be held in uniformity; they don't have the same structure, processes, or impact and shouldn't be positioned as the be-all and end-all solutions.

The technologies discussed differ significantly from the ones touted by proponents of geoengineering, who want to, for example, shoot dust into the atmosphere to reflect the sun's radiation. While these suggestions are no doubt a creative outlet, they give technology solutions grounded in reality a bad wrap.

We must also tap into different ways of thinking, including grassroots and Indigenous experiences that may challenge how we've been taught to understand the world. Meanwhile, we can't just follow the solutions that can make economic profit and instead begin to measure social outcomes at scale. For the climate tools that are adopted, their nuances must be understood too.

When we begin to tell better truths, we can come together, collaborate, and fight against the crisis. While we have likely passed and are dangerously close to some environmental tipping points, we should also be nearing social tipping points, where society can pressure governments to make change, as it did with the creation of national parks.

People sometimes dispute the role of technology in fighting the climate crisis. Fundamentally, though, we are all in the same camp. There shouldn't be a "this or that" debate. Of course, there is some uncertainty around what the future brings, so we must compare technologies and ensure that every pound we invest goes to the highest probability of significant impact rather than just seeing what sticks. What will help us is technology being cheap and fast.

Not all technologies discussed in this book intend to cut emissions, many help restore biodiversity and ecosystems and facilitate broader change. To reduce carbon emissions, we need to stop burning fossil fuels. It's as easy as that.

Clean Up on Aisle Earth attempts to show how technology can drive climate action. As you turn the last page, remember you are crucial to the climate puzzle. Your actions, no matter how small, can contribute to the collective effort to close current gaps. Many people opt not to attend traditional protests or direct action. Still, you can write to your MP or local representative, speak to your neighbours, or switch to clean energy from a small renewables co-op. The next step is determining what is possible for you and how you fit into the climate puzzle to make that impact. Your individual actions matter, and together they can make a significant difference.

It's about being active, not necessarily an activist. Collective action is one of the most potent forces for systemic change. Tech is just a tool – the most powerful tool we've ever had – but it will be good or bad depending on its use. Let's make sure it's the former.

References

1 "Global Climate Highlights 2024." *Copernicus*, 10 January 2025.climate.copernicus.eu/global-climate-highlights-2024. Accessed 28 May 2025.

2 "Cleaning up couture: what's in your jeans?" *UN Environment Programme*, 14 December 2018. unep.org/news-and-stories/story/cleaning-couture-whats-your-jeans. Accessed 20 June 2025.

3 "Revealed: Big tech's new datacentres will take water from the world's driest areas." Luke Barratt, Costanza Gambarini, Andrew Witherspoon, Aliya Uteuova, *The Guardian*, 9 April 2025. theguardian.com/environment/2025/apr/09/big-tech-datacentres-water. Accessed 6 July 2025.

4 Benjamin Sovacool, personal interview, 26 June 2024.

5 "Net Zero Economy Index 2024." *PWC*. pwc.co.uk/services/sustainability-climate-change/insights/net-zero-economy-index.html. Accessed 28 May 2025.

6 "World's top climate scientists expect global heating to blast past 1.5C target." Damian Carrington, *The Guardian*, 8 May 2024. theguardian.com/environment/article/2024/may/08/world-scientists-climate-failure-survey-global-temperature. Accessed 28 May 2025.

7 "How Close Are the Planet's Climate Tipping Points?" *The New York Times*, 11 August 2024. nytimes.com/inter-

active/2024/08/11/climate/earth-warming-climate-tipping-points.html. Accessed 28 May 2025.

8 "Table of Solutions." *Project Drawdown*. drawdown.org/solutions/table-of-solutions. Accessed 28 May 2025.

9 "ExxonMobil: Oil giant predicted climate change in 1970s – scientists." Georgina Rannard, BBC News, 12 January 2023. bbc.co.uk/news/science-environment-64241994. Accessed 28 May 2025.

10 "Shell and Exxon's secret 1980s climate change warnings." Benjamin Franta, *The Guardian*, 19 September 2018. theguardian.com/environment/climate-consensus-97-per-cent/2018/sep/19/shell-and-exxons-secret-1980s-climate-change-warnings. Accessed 28 May 2025.

11 "BP knew the truth about climate change 30 years ago. Now, it's time to ban fossil industry advertising." *Follow the Money*, 26 May 2020. Accessed 28 May 2025. ftm.eu/articles/bp-video-climate-change-1990-engels.

12 "Over $50 Billion Flow to Climate-Tech Startups in a Stormy Year." Musfika Mishi, BloombergNEF, 13 February 2024. about.bnef.com/blog/over-50-billion-flow-to-climate-tech-startups-in-a-stormy-year/. Accessed 28 May 2025.

13 "Fossil Fuel Subsidies Surged to Record $7 Trillion." Simon Black, Ian Parry, Nate Vernon-Lin, IMF, 24 August 2023. imf.org/en/Blogs/Articles/2023/08/24/fossil-fuel-subsidies-surged-to-record-7-trillion. Accessed 28 May 2025.

14 "The $7 Trillion a Year Needed to Hit Net-Zero Goal." *BloombergNEF*, 7 December 2022. about.bnef.com/blog/the-7-trillion-a-year-needed-to-hit-net-zero-goal/. Accessed 28 May 2025.

15 "The Port of Tyne." *The Chartered Institution of Highways and Transportation*. ciht.org.uk/media/8088/the_port_of_tyne.pdf. Accessed 28 May 2025.

16 "Climate change: atmospheric carbon dioxide." Rebecca Lindsey, *Climate*, 21 May 2025. climate.gov/news-features/understanding-climate/climate-change-atmospheric-carbon-dioxide. Accessed 28 May 2025.

17 CO2.earth/daily-CO2. Accessed 30 May 2025.

18 "Strong evidence shows Sixth Mass Extinction of global biodiversity in progress." University of Hawaii, *Science Daily*, 13 January 2022. sciencedaily.com/releases/2022/01/220113194911.htm. Accessed 28 May 2025.

19 "Overview of Greenhouse Gases." *Environmental Protection Agency*. epa.gov/ghgemissions/overview-greenhouse-gases. Accessed 29 June 2025.

20 "Darlington Forest Project plants trees to combat climate crisis." Tasmin Lockwood, *The Northern Echo,* 14 February 2020. thenorthernecho.co.uk/news/local/darlington/18234308.darlington-forest-project-plants-trees-combat-climate-crisis/. Accessed 29 June 2025.

21 "Diverse forests hold huge carbon potential, as long as we cut emissions." ETH Zurich, *Phys*, 13 November 2023. phys.org/news/2023-11-diverse-forests-huge-carbon-potential.html. Accessed 28 May 2025.

22 "Half of the world's habitable land is used for agriculture." Hannah Ritchie, Max Roser, *Our World in Data*, 16 February 2024. ourworldindata.org/global-land-for-agriculture. Accessed 28 May 2025.

23 "The ocean – the world's greatest ally against climate change." United Nations. un.org/en/climatechange/science/climate-issues/ocean. Accessed 28 May 2025.

24 "Pathways to Unblocking Private Financing for Nature-based Solutions." Sheccid Gómez, Valeria López Portillo Purata and Sarai Eunice Rodríguez, *Work Resources Institute,* 23 February 2023. wri.org/update/pathways-unblocking-private-financing-nature-based-solutions. Accessed 29 June 2025.

25 *Frontier*. frontierclimate.com/. Accessed 28 May 2025.

26 "Which form of transport has the smallest carbon footprint?" Hannah Ritchie, *Our World In Data*. 30 August 2023. ourworldindata.org/travel-carbon-footprint. Accessed 29 June 2025. The article data reveals that conventional trains, trams and coaches have a lower carbon footprint than even electric cars, but average buses did not. No data on electric buses was not reality available.

27 "In the Race to Electrification, the Humble Bus Is in the Lead." Kyle Stock, *Bloomberg*. 9 June 2023.

bloomberg.com/news/articles/2023-06-09/buses-are-going-electric-faster-than-passenger-cars. Accessed 29 June 2025.

28 I acknowledge that the terms "Global South" and "Global North" are reductively general and are used here hesitantly for lack of better alternatives.

29 "In Cambodia, Indigenous villagers lose forest & land amid carbon offset project." Jack Brook, *Mongabay*, 24 July 2024. news.mongabay.com/2024/07/in-cambodia-Indigenous-villagers-lose-forest-land-amid-carbon-offset-project/. Accessed 28 May 2025.

30 "Farmers hold 'tractor run' in pylon protest." *BBC News*, 22 April 2024. bbc.co.uk/news/articles/c88zk2z70r0o. Accessed 28 May 2025.

31 "How to Prevent City Climate Action from Becoming "Green Gentrification"." Maria Hart, Jillian Du, Caroline Coccoli, *World Resources Institute*, 12 December 2019. wri.org/insights/how-prevent-city-climate-action-becoming-green-gentrification. Accessed 28 May 2025.

32 "Sources of opposition to renewable energy projects in the United States." Lawrence Susskind, Jungwoo Chun, Alexander Gant, Chelsea Hodgkins, Jessica Cohen, Sarah Lohmar, Energy Policy, Volume 165, 2022, 112922, ISSN

0301-4215, https://doi.org/10.1016/j.enpol.2022.112922. Accessed 28 May 2025.

33 "Project Drawdown presents the Drawdown Roadmap: The Five Parts of the Drawdown Roadmap | Unit 3." Project Drawdown, *YouTube*, 26 April 2023. youtube.com/watch?v=xSvQYMH3FJw&list=PLwYnpej4pQF5-5LMWplNNz9TNdFrOZ2R2&index=4. Accessed 28 May 2025.

34 "Amazon forest felled to build road for climate summit." *BBC,* 12 March 2025. bbc.co.uk/news/articles/c9vy191rgn1o. Accessed on 20 June 2025.

35 The State of Carbon Dioxide Removal. stateofcdr.org/. Accessed 28 May 2025.

36 "IPCC Unsummarized: Unmasking Clear Warnings on Overshoot, Techno-fixes, and the Urgency of Climate Justice." *Center for International Environmental Law*. ciel.org/reports/ipcc-wg3-briefing/. Accessed 28 May 2025.

37 Ben Rubin, personal interview, 18 June 2024.

38 "Climeworks switches on world's largest direct air capture plant." *Climeworks*, 8 May 2024. climeworks.com/press-release/climeworks-switches-on-worlds-largest-direct-air-capture-plant-mammoth. Accessed 28 May 2025.

39 "Climeworks' capture fails to cover its own emissions." Bjartmar Oddur Þeyr Alexandersson and Valur Grettisson, *Heimildin*. 15 May 2025. heimildin.is/grein/24581/climeworks-capture-fails-to-cover-its-own-emissions/. Accessed 29 June 2025.

40 Mark Jacobson, *LinkedIn*. linkedin.com/posts/mark-jacobson-1b58b38_climeworks-capture-fails-to-cover-its-own-activity-7328803057138368513-GR5j. Accessed 29 June 2025.

41 Mark Jacobson, personal email, 19 August 2025.

42 "Stanford study casts doubt on carbon capture." Taylor Kubota, *Stanford University*, 25 October 2019. news.stanford.edu/stories/2019/10/study-casts-doubt-carbon-capture. Accessed 28 May 2025.

43 "Energy system of Kenya." *IEA*. iea.org/countries/kenya. Accessed 28 May 2025.

44 Personal interview. Bilha Ndirangu. 27 June 2024.

45 "US DOE's DAC hubs advancing under Trump administration." Brandon Mulder, Carbon Pulse, 18 March 2025. carbon-pulse.com/378782/. Accessed 28 May 2025.

46 "45Q Tax Credit Update: Impacts to Carbon Capture Investment." Jamison Braun, FactSet, 22 August 2025. insight.factset.com/45q-tax-credit-update-impacts-to-carbon-capture-investment. Accessed 23 August 2025.

47 "U.S. cleantech spending benefits marginalized communities." Amena H. Saiyid, *cipher*, 17 July 2024. ciphernews.com/articles/u-s-cleantech-spending-benefits-marginalized-communities/. Accessed 28 May 2025.

48 "Carbon Capture and Storage: History and the Road Ahead." Jinfeng Ma, Lin Li, Haofan Wang, Yi Du, Junjie Ma, Xiaoli Zhang, Zhenliang Wang, *Engineering*, Volume 14, 2022, Pages 33-43, ISSN 2095-8099, doi.org/10.1016/j.eng.2021.11.024.

49 "Global Carbon Capture Capacity Due to Rise Sixfold by 2030." *BloombergNEF*, 18 October 2022. about.bnef.com/blog/global-carbon-capture-capacity-due-to-rise-sixfold-by-2030/. Accessed 28 May 2025.

50 "Big Oil's climate targets" *Reuters*, 1 April 2025. reuters.com/sustainability/climate-energy/big-oils-climate-targets-2024-11-12/. Accessed on 20 June 2025.

51 "Public engagement and collaboration for carbon dioxide removal: lessons from a project in the Dominican Republic." Hilser Harry, Hiraldo Lia, Moreau Cheyenne, Draiby Andrea, Cox Emily, Andrews M. Grace, Winks Lewis, Walworth Nathan G. Frontiers in Climate, Volume 6 – 2024, 2624-9553 frontiersin.org/journals/climate/articles/10.3389/fclim.2024.1290999.

52 "NASA | A Year in the Life of Earth's CO2." NASA Goddard, *YouTube*, 17 November 2014. youtube.com/watch?v=x1SgmFa0r04. Accessed 29 June 2025.

53 "Our mission." 1t.org/about-us/ Accessed 29 June 2025.

54 "Climate Finance Thematic Briefing: REDD+ Finance." Charlene Watson, Liane Schalatek, *Climate Funds Update*, February 2020. climatefundsupdate.org/wp-content/uploads/2020/03/CFF5-2019-ENG-DIGITAL.pdf. Accessed 28 May 2025.

55 "Recognizing Indigenous Peoples' land interests is critical for people and nature." *WWF*, 22 October 2020. worldwildlife.org/stories/recognizing-Indigenous-peoples-land-interests-is-critical-for-people-and-nature. Accessed 28 May 2025.

56 "Implementing the ILO Indigenous and Tribal Peoples Convention No. 169: Towards an inclusive, sustainable and just future." Rishabh Kumar Dhir, Umberto Cattaneo, Maria Victoria Cabrera Ormaza, Hernan Coronado, Martin Oelz, *International Labour Organization*, 3 February 2020. ilo.org/publications/implementing-ilo-Indigenous-and-tribal-peoples-convention-no-169-towards. Accessed 28 May 2025.

57 "Inside the fight against illegal mining in the Amazon." Chris Greenberg, *Greenpeace*, 10 April 2023. greenpeace.org/international/story/59123/amazon-rainforest-mining-illegal/. Accessed 28 May 2025.

58 "Replacing the forest with plantations." *WWF*. wwf.panda.org/discover/knowledge_hub/where_we_work/amazon/amazon_threats/mechanized_agriculture/. Accessed 28 May 2025.

59 "Closing the Climate Data Divide in the Global South." Juan Lavista Ferres, Microsoft, 7 November 2022. blogs.microsoft.com/on-the-issues/2022/11/07/climate-data-divide-global-south/. Accessed 28 May 2025.

60 "Synthesis of magnetic biochar from agricultural waste biomass to enhancing route for waste water and polymer application: A review." K.R. Thines, E.C. Abdullah, N.M. Mubarak, M. Ruthiraan, *Renewable and Sustainable Energy Reviews*, Volume 67, 2017, Pages 257-276, ISSN 1364-0321, doi.org/10.1016/j.rser.2016.09.057.

61 Osman, A.I., Farghali, M., Dong, Y. *et al.* Reducing the carbon footprint of buildings using biochar-based bricks and insulating materials: a review. *Environ Chem Lett* 22, 71–104 (2024). https://doi.org/10.1007/s10311-023-01662-7.

62 "Understanding Biochar Permanence: Balancing Conservatism and Uncertainty." Syakira Yazan, Simon Manley, Sylvera, 14 April 2025. sylvera.com/blog/understanding-biochar-permanence-balancing-conservatism-and-uncertainty. Accessed 31 May 2025.

63 "Research Shows Biochar May Be Durable For More Than 1000 Years". Petya Trendafoliva, *Carbon Herald*, 22 March 2023. carbonherald.com/research-shows-biochar-may-be-durable-for-more-than-1000-years/. Accessed 23 August 2025.

64 "Leaderboards". CDR.fyi. cdr.fyi/leaderboards. Accessed 29 June 2025.

65 "Biochar for a sustainable future: Environmentally friendly production and diverse applications." *Science Direct*, September 2024. sciencedirect.com/science/article/pii/S2590123024006881#bib22. Accessed 20 June 2025.

66 "Planboo activates a bamboo biochar project in Thailand." *Planboo*, 21 September 2023. youtube.com/watch?v=iuBS5HjHSQI. Accessed 28 May 2025.

67 Personal interview, Jim Mann, 3 July 2024.

68 "Revealed: more than 90% of rainforest carbon offsets by biggest certifier are worthless, analysis shows." Patric Greenfield, *The Guardian*. 18 January 2023. theguardian.com/environment/2023/jan/18/revealed-forest-carbon-offsets-biggest-provider-worthless-verra-aoe. Accessed 29 June 2025.

69 Personal interview, Hans Westerhof, 17 June 2024.

70 "New research: Carbon credits are associated with businesses decarbonizing faster." Ecosystem Marketplace. ecosystemmarketplace.com/articles/new-research-carbon-credits-are-associated-with-businesses-decarbonizing-faster/. Accessed 28 May 2025.

71 "COP28: Climate finance." *McKinsey Sustainability*,4 December 2023. mckinsey.com/capabilities/sustainability/our-insights/sustainability-blog/cop28-climate-finance. Accessed 28 May 2025.

72 "Coal Miners (Retraining)." UK Parliament. 30 November 1993. hansard.parliament.uk/commons/1993-11-30/debates/4bd4ea64-e0c4-47c1-a6e5-bb8f2098335a/CoalMiners(Retraining). Accessed 28 May 2025.

73 "Job displacement costs of phasing out coal." Juan-Pablo Rud, Michael Simmons, Gerhard Toews, Fernando Aragon, *Institute for Fiscal Studies*. ifs.org.uk/sites/default/files/2022-09/Job%20displacement%20costs%20of%20phasing%20out%20coal.pdf. Accessed 28 May 2025.

74 "Al Gore's Speech On Renewable Energy." *NPR*, 17 July 2008. npr.org/2008/07/17/92638501/al-gores-speech-on-renewable-energy. Accessed 28 May 2025.

75 "United States. Sources of electricity generation." *IEA*,

2023. iea.org/countries/united-states/electricity. Accessed 30 June 2025.

76 “Renewables.” *IEA*. iea.org/energy-system/renewables. Accessed 30 June 2025.

77 “Greenhouse Gas Emissions from Energy Data Explorer.” *IEA*, 2 August 2024. iea.org/data-and-statistics/data-tools/greenhouse-gas-emissions-from-energy-data-explorer. Accessed 28 May 2025.

78 “For the first time in decades, the number of people without access to electricity is set to increase in 2022.” Laura Cozzi, Daniel Wetzel, Gianluca Tonolo, Jacob Hyppolite II, IEA, 3 November 2022. iea.org/commentaries/for-the-first-time-in-decades-the-number-of-people-without-access-to-electricity-is-set-to-increase-in-2022. Accessed 31 May 2025.

79 “Climate change.” *WHO,* 12 October 2023. https://www.who.int/news-room/fact-sheets/detail/climate-change-and-health Accessed 30 June 2025.

80 “Revealed: Saudi Arabia’s grand plan to ‘hook’ poor countries on oil.” Damian Carrington, *The Guardian*. 27 November 2023. theguardian.com/environment/2023/nov/27/revealed-saudi-arabia-plan-poor-countries-oil. Accessed 29 July 2025.

81 “The Global South is surging ahead in the renewables revolution.” Vikram Singh, *Climate Home News.* 16 October 2024. climatechangenews.com/2024/10/16/the-global-south-is-surging-ahead-in-the-renewables-revolution/. Accessed 30 June 2025.

82 “Will the green transition be globally just, or a neocolonial resource grab? Trade rules are key.” Cleodie Rickard, *Global Justice Now*, 22 May 2024. globaljustice.org.uk/blog/2024/05/will-the-green-transition-be-globally-just-or-a-neocolonial-resource-grab-trade-rules-are-key/. Accessed 30 June 2025.

83 "Hydroelectricity." *IEA*. iea.org/energy-system/renewables/hydroelectricity. Accessed 28 May 2025.

84 "Their Land Was Drowned by a Flood of Hydropower." Zoë Yunker, The Tyee, 19 April 2022. thetyee.ca/News/2022/04/19/Their-Land-Was-Drowned-By-A-Flood-Of-Hydropower/. Accessed 28 May 2025.

85 "Hunger numbers stubbornly high for three consecutive years as global crises deepen: UN report." *WHO*, 24 July 2024. who.int/news/item/24-07-2024-hunger-numbers-stubbornly-high-for-three-consecutive-years-as-global-crises-deepen--un-report. Accessed 28 May 2025.

86 "Drax: UK power station still burning rare forest wood." Joe Crowley, *BBC*. 28 February 2024. bbc.co.uk/news/science-environment-68381160. Accessed 30 June 2025.

87 "When Edison Lit Up Manhattan." *The New York Historical*, 4 September 2014. nyhistory.org/blogs/edison-lit-manhattan. Accessed 28 May 2025.

88 "Octopus Power Pack: the UK's first Vehicle-to-Grid tariff." Octopus Energy. octopus.energy/power-pack/#V2Gsignup. Accessed 30 June 2025.

89 "Policy Brief: Grid capacity needs to more than double by 2035 to meet the EU's Paris Agreement Goals." *PAC*. pac-scenarios.eu/news/detail/news/policy-brief-grid-capacity-needs-to-more-than-double-by-2035-to-meet-the-eus-paris-agreement-goals.html. Accessed 28 May 2025.

90 "Recent developments in multifunctional coatings for solar panel applications: A review." Mohammad Sayem Mozumder, Abdel-Hamid I. Mourad, Hifsa Pervez, Riham Surkatti, *Solar Energy Materials and Solar Cells*, Volume 189, 2019, Pages 75-102, ISSN 0927-0248, doi.org/10.1016/j.solmat.2018.09.015.

91 "Oxford PV sets new solar panel efficiency world record." Oxford PV. 31 January 2024. oxfordpv.com/news/oxford-pv-sets-new-solar-panel-efficiency-world-record-0 Accessed 30 June 2025.

92 "How Germany outfitted half a million balconies with solar panels." Akielly Hu, *Grist*, 26 September 2024. grist.org/buildings/how-germany-outfitted-half-a-million-balconies-with-solar-panels/. Accessed 28 May 2025.

93 Personal interview, Shirley Pazos Bashualdo. 13 August 2024.

94 "Vanishing Trees and Lakes: Deforestation in Bolivia's Amazon." Juan Diego Cárdenas, *Climate Diplomacy*, 22 May 2024. climate-diplomacy.org/magazine/environment/vanishing-trees-and-lakes-deforestation-bolivias-amazon. Accessed 28 May 2025.

95 "Protected Areas: Illegal Timber Strongholds in the Bolivian Amazon." Juan Diego Cárdenas, Seth Robbins, *Climate Diplomacy*, 31 May 2024. climate-diplomacy.org/magazine/environment/protected-areas-illegal-timber-strongholds-bolivian-amazon. Accessed 28 May 2025.

96 "Growing Energy Co-operatives - United Kingdom of Great Britain and Northern Ireland." *United Nations Climate Change*. unfccc.int/climate-action/momentum-for-change/activity-database/growing-energy-co-operatives. Accessed 28 May 2025.

97 "Community Energy in Italy." *Patagonia*. eu.patagonia.com/pl/en/wethepower/getinvolved/italy/. Accessed 28 May 2025.

98 "A new era for rural electric cooperatives: New clean energy investments, supported by federal incentives, will reduce rates, emissions, and reliance on outside power." Nikit Abhyankar, Umed Paliwal, Michael O'Boyle, Michelle Solomon, Jeremy Fisher, Amol Phadke, *The Electricity Jour-*

nal, Volume 36, Issue 8, 2023, 107334, ISSN 1040-6190, https://doi.org/10.1016/j.tej.2023.107334.

99 "Empowering people – the role of local energy communities in clean energy transitions." Vida Rozite, Matthieu Prin, Silvia Laera, Josh Oxby, Alexandre Roussel, *IEA*. iea.org/commentaries/empowering-people-the-role-of-local-energy-communities-in-clean-energy-transitions. Accessed 28 May 2025.

100 "Annual Fuel Poverty Statistics in England, 2024 (2023 data)." Department for Energy Security and Net Zero, 15 February 2024. assets.publishing.service.gov.uk/media/65ccecba1d939500129466a9/annual-fuel-poverty-statistics-report-2024.pdf. Accessed 29 May 2025.

101 "Electricity Prices in Thailand: Insights and Tips 2025." Kristian, *Thailand Simple*, 16 October 2023. thailandsimple.com/electricity-prices-in-thailand/. Accessed 29 May 2025.

102 Benjamin Sovacool, personal interview, 26 June 2024.

103 "FAQ's", Ripple. rippleenergy.com/faq/the-co-op. Accessed 29 May 2025.

104 "Lack of ambition and attention risks making electricity grids the weak link in clean energy transitions." *IEA*, 17 October 2023. iea.org/news/lack-of-ambition-and-attention-risks-making-electricity-grids-the-weak-link-in-clean-energy-transitions. Accessed 29 May 2025.

105 "Inflation Reduction Act." U.S. Department of Energy. energy.gov/gdo/inflation-reduction-act. Accessed 29 May 2025.

106 "Trump Is Freezing Money for Clean Energy. Red States Have the Most to Lose." Lisa Friedman, Brad Plumer, Harry Stevens, *The New York Times*, 10 February 2025. nytimes.com/2025/02/10/climate/trump-clean-energy-republican-states.html. Accessed 29 May 2025.

107 "EU invests over € 1 billion in energy infrastructure in support of the Green Deal." *European Commission*, 26 January 2022. commission.europa.eu/news/eu-invests-over-eu-1-billion-energy-infrastructure-support-green-deal-2022-01-26_en. Accessed 29 May 2025.

108 "Bezos-Backed Group to Prepare South African Grids for Investment." Bloomberg, *Energy Connects*, 16 September 2024. energyconnects.com/news/renewables/2024/september/bezos-backed-group-to-prepare-south-african-grids-for-investment/. Accessed 29 May 2025.

109 "Transform project planning with AI-powered technology." *Continuum Industries*. continuum.industries/product/optioneer. Accessed 29 May 2025.

110 "U.S tech giants are building dozens of data centers in Chile. Locals are fighting back." Claudia Urquieta, Daniela Dib, *Rest of World*. 31 May 2024. restofworld.org/2024/data-centers-environmental-issues/. Accessed 30 June 2025.

111 "Popular information." *The Nobel Prize*. nobelprize.org/prizes/chemistry/2019/popular-information/. Accessed 29 May 2025.

112 "The Indigenous groups fighting against the quest for 'white gold'." Berta Reventós, *BBC News*, 27 August 2023. bbc.com/news/world-latin-america-66520097. Accessed 29 July 2025.

113 "Cobalt mines – child labour in the Democratic Republic of the Congo." Tomáš Zdechovský, European Parliament, 17 June 2022. europarl.europa.eu/doceo/document/E-9-2022-002207_EN.html. Accessed 29 May 2025.

114 "Projects." Northern Lithium. northernlithium.co.uk/ludwell-farm-borehole-1/. Accessed 30 May 2025.

115 "Heat accounted for almost half of total final energy consumption and 38% of energy-related CO2 emissions in

2022." *IEA*. iea.org/reports/renewables-2023/heat. Accessed 30 May 2025.

116 "Warming up to district heating and thermal solar." Tasmin Lockwood, *Digital Frontier*, 19 June 2025. digitalfrontier.com/articles/warming-district-heating-thermal-solar. Accessed 1 July 2025.

117 Christophe Williams, personal interview, 19 August 2025.

118 "A battery swap scheme is turning Africa's roads electric." Nell Lewis, *CNN*. https://edition.cnn.com/2023/09/04/africa/spiro-battery-swap-africa-electric-bikes-spc-intl. Accessed 22 August 2025.

119 "Geothermal." *Government of Iceland.* government.is/topics/business-and-industry/energy/geothermal/. Accessed 1 July 2025.

120 "The History of Geothermal Energy." *Morrison Inc.* morrisongeothermal.com/the-history-of-geothermal-energy/. Accessed 30 May 2025.

121 "First SDH system in Sub-Saharan Africa." *Solar Thermal World*, 22 May 2019. solarthermalworld.org/news/first-sdh-system-sub-saharan-africa/. Accessed 30 May 2025.

122 "France's clean power clout to be tested again this winter." Gavin Maguire, *Reuters*, 8 November 2023. reuters.com/markets/commodities/frances-clean-power-clout-be-tested-again-this-winter-2023-11-08/. Accessed 30 May 2025.

123 "Germany has shut down its last three nuclear power plants, and some climate scientists are aghast." Catherine Clifford, *CNBC*, 18 April 2023. cnbc.com/2023/04/18/germany-shuts-down-last-nuclear-power-plants-some-scientists-aghast.html. Accessed 30 May 2025.

124 Sovacool, Benjamin K., The Political Economy of Energy

Poverty: A Review of Key Challenges (August 30, 2011). Energy for Sustainable Development 16 (2012) 272–282, Available at SSRN: https://ssrn.com/abstract=3445414. Accessed 30 May 2025.

125 "A mixed tapestry of crops saves land and produces more protein than monocultures." Emma Bryce, *Anthropocene Magazine*. 20 January 2023. anthropocenemagazine.org/2023/01/landmark-analysis-of-132-studies-highlights-the-true-power-of-intercropping-on-farms/. Accessed 1 July 2025.

126 "2023 Environmental Update." *The Coca-Cola Company*. coca-colacompany.com/content/dam/company/us/en/reports/2023-environmental-update/2023-environmental-update.pdf. Accessed 30 May 2025.

127 "Half of World's GDP Moderately or Highly Dependent on Nature, Says New Report." Amanda Russo, *World Economic Forum*, 19 January 2020. weforum.org/press/2020/01/half-of-world-s-gdp-moderately-or-highly-dependent-on-nature-says-new-report/. Accessed 30 May 2025.

128 "MEASURING PROGRESS?." Tim Jackson, Nat McBride, *Centre for Environmental Strategy, University of Surrey*, 2005. surrey.ac.uk/sites/default/files/2018-03/11-05-measuring-progress-final.pdf. Accessed 30 May 2025.

129 "'Nature is taking back Venice': wildlife returns to tourist-free city." John Brunton, *The Guardian*, 20 March 2020. theguardian.com/environment/2020/mar/20/nature-is-taking-back-venice-wildlife-returns-to-tourist-free-city. Accessed 30 May 2025.

130 "A trio of 'jackass' penguins were caught waddling around the streets of Cape Town during lockdown." Qayyah Moynihan, Helena Wasserman, Business Insider, 20 April 2020. businessinsider.com/three-animals-african-penguins-south-africa-social-distancing-2020-4. Accessed 1 June 2025.

131 "Llandudno marauders: the herd of goats running riot through a Welsh town" *The Guardian*, 31 March 2020. theguardian.com/news/2020/mar/31/llandudno-goats-herd-running-riot-coronavirus-lockdown. Accessed 20 June 2025.

132 "Nurture to nature via COVID-19, a self-regenerating environmental strategy of environment in global context." *National Library of Medicine,* 29 April 2020. pmc.ncbi.nlm.nih.gov/articles/PMC7189854/#bb0370. Accessed 20 June 2025.

133 "The COVID-19 pandemic is not a break for nature – let's make sure there is one after the crisis." Sebastian Troëng, Edward B Barbier, Carlos Manuel Rodríguez Echandi, World Economic Forum, 21 May 2020. weforum.org/stories/2020/05/covid-19-coronavirus-pandemic-nature-environment-green-stimulus-biodiversity/. Accessed 1 June 2025.

134 "Vampire hedgehogs, pirate spiders and fishy fungi - the strangest new species of 2024." Frankie Adkins, *BBC*, 29 December 2024. bbc.co.uk/future/article/20241224-the-new-plant-and-animal-species-discovered-in-2024. Accessed 30 May 2025.

135 "CSDDD | Updates, Compliance." *CSDDD.* corporate-sustainability-due-diligence-directive.com/. Accessed 30 May 2025.

136 "Nature Restoration Regulation." *European Commission.* environment.ec.europa.eu/topics/nature-and-biodiversity/nature-restoration-law_en. Accessed 30 May 2025.

137 "Kunming-Montreal Global Biodiversity Framework." Convention on Biological Diversity, *UN*, 19 December 2022. unep.org/resources/kunming-montreal-global-biodiversity-framework. Accessed 30 May 2025.

138 "A New Deal to Close the Nature Finance Gap." The Nature Conservancy, 22 September 2021. nature.org/en-us/what-we-do/our-insights/perspectives/closing-nature-finance-gap-cbd/. Accessed 30 May 2025.

139 "Sky skimmers: The race to fly satellites in the lowest orbits yet." Jonathan O'Callaghan, *BBC*, 9 February 2025. bbc.com/future/article/20250207-sky-skimmers-the-race-to-send-satellites-into-very-low-earth-orbits. Accessed 30 May 2025.

140 "Starlink simulation and potential analysis for remote sensing applications." Yang, Hai Tao, Wang, HaoYu, Lv, Bo, Wang, JinYu, Zhou, Xi Xuan, Zhang, Hong Gang. Proceedings of the SPIE, Volume 12976, id. 129761A 18 pp. (2023). December 2023. 10.1117/12.3009125.

141 "Small Language Models Gaining Popularity While LLMs Still Go Strong." Lance Elliot, *Forbes*. 8 November 2024. forbes.com/sites/lanceeliot/2024/11/08/small-language-models-slm-gaining-popularity-while-large-language-models-llm-still-going-strong-and-reaching-for-the-stars/. Accessed 02 July 2025.

142 "Life below water." *UNEP.* 7 June 2021. unep.org/interactives/status-world-coral-reefs/. Accessed 5 July 2025.

143 Levy, Natalie & Berman, Ofer & Yuval, Matan & Loya, Yossi & Treibitz, Tali & Tarazi, Ezri & Levy, Oren. (2022). Emerging 3D technologies for future reformation of coral reefs: Enhancing biodiversity using biomimetic structures based on designs by nature. Science of The Total Environment. 830. 10.1016/j.scitotenv.2022.154749.

144 "Ocean acidification is destroying coral reefs. Here's how 2 scientists are using bone research to protect them against climate change." Tasmin Lockwood, *Business Insider*. 26 April 2023. businessinsider.com/ocean-acidification-bone-research-predict-reef-health-2023-4.
Accessed 5 July 2025.

145 "Epistemic pluralism and climate change." *The London School of Economics*. lse.ac.uk/Events/2025/03/202503101830/Epistemic-pluralism-and-climate-change. Accessed 5 July 2025.

146 "Climate Action 30." *Business Insider*. 27 November 2023. businessinsider.com/climate-action-30-global-leaders-climate-solutions-2023-11#nouhad-awwad-umah-for-earth-campaigner-and-global-outreach-coordinator-greenpeace-mena-7. Accessed 5 July 2025.

147 Tara Houska, Personal interview, 2023.

148 Tara Houska, Personal message, 14 August 2024.

149 "Biomimicry – The Burr and the Invention of Velcro." Micro Photonics Inc. microphotonics.com/biomimicry-burr-invention-velcro/. Accessed 30 May 2025.

150 "Whale biomimicry inspires better wind turbines." Mongabay, 7 July 2008. news.mongabay.com/2008/07/whale-biomimicry-inspires-better-wind-turbines/. Accessed 30 May 2025.

151 From an email titled. "Economic Case for Climate Action".

152 "The CAT Thermometer explained." *Climate Action Tracker.* climateactiontracker.org/global/cat-thermometer/. Accessed 30 May 2025.

153 "A brief history of GDP - and what could come next." Peter Vanham, *World Economic Forum*, 13 December 2021. weforum.org/stories/2021/12/stakeholder-capitalism-episode-1-a-brief-history-of-gdp. Accessed 30 May 2025.

154 "IPCC Must Include More Global South Scientists, Indigenous and Traditional Knowledge Holders." Adam Markham, The Equation, 29 January 2024. blog.ucs.org/adam-markham/ipcc-must-include-more-global-south-

scientists-Indigenous-and-traditional-knowledge-holders/. Accessed 30 May 2025.

155 "About the Santiago Network." *United Nations*. unfccc.int/santiago-network/about. Accessed 30 May 2025.

156 "China is leading the way in electrification, too." Nick Hedley, *The Progress Playbook*, 19 June 2024. theprogressplaybook.com/2024/06/19/china-is-leading-the-way-in-electrification-too/. Accessed 30 May 2025.

157 "Executive summary." *IEA*. iea.org/reports/denmark-2023/executive-summary. Accessed 30 May 2025.

158 "Wind Energy in Denmark." *United Nations*. unfccc.int/ttclear/misc_/StaticFiles/gnwoerk_static/TEC_NSI/63eb6ced5b1e43429a6eccdef95ff61e/85bd141304c5486fb7f2ef71f8d2d45f.pdf. Accessed 30 May 2025.

159 "Fossil Fuel Subsidies." *International Monetary Fund*. imf.org/en/Topics/climate-change/energy-subsidies#. Accessed 30 May 2025.

160 "About the fund." Norges Bank Investment Management. nbim.no/en/about-us/about-the-fund/. Accessed 30 May 2025.

161 "Norway wealth fund posts record $222 billion profit but warns tech boom won't last. Gwladys Fouche, *Reuters*, 29 January 2025. reuters.com/business/finance/norway-wealth-fund-posts-record-222-bln-annual-profit-tech-boom-2025-01-29/. Accessed 30 May 2025.

162 "Executive summary." *IEA*. iea.org/reports/norway-2022/executive-summary. Accessed 30 May 2025.

163 "'Not every Norwegian feels guilty but many do'." Jorn Madslien, *BBC News*, 29 July 2024. bbc.co.uk/news/articles/cz5r2mk18k1o. Accessed 30 May 2025.

164 "Community Benefits Agreements: A New Local Government Tool or Another Variation on the Exactions Theme?." Vicki Been, *The University of Chicago Law Review*, 77:5 2010.

chicagounbound.uchicago.edu/cgi/viewcontent.cgi?article=5489&context=uclrev. Accessed 30 May 2025.

165 Liz Wall and Fiona Haslam McKenzie, "Time for an Outcome Evaluation? The Experience of Indigenous Communities with Mining Benefit Sharing Agreements", *International Development Policy | Revue internationale de politique de développement* [Online], 15 | 2023, Online since 02 May 2023, connection on 30 May 2025. URL: http://journals.openedition.org/poldev/5365; DOI: https://doi.org/10.4000/poldev.5365.

166 "Rollback: Trump Rescinded Biden's Executive Order 14008 Establishing Justice40 Initiative." Environmental & Energy Law Program Harvard Law School. 20 January 2025. eelp.law.harvard.edu/tracker/rollback-trump-rescinded-bidens-executive-order-14008-that-established-justice40-initiative/. Accessed 30 May 2025.

167 "Introduction." *GCR*. globalcarbonreward.org/introduction/. Accessed 30 May 2025.

168 Delton Chen, personal emails. 22 August 2025.

169 "The importance of ecological economics: An interview with Herman Daly." Herman Daly, Jamie Morgan, real-world economics review, Issue 90, 2019. paecon.net/PAEReview/issue90/DalyMorgan90.pdf. Accessed 30 May 2025.

170 Ibid.

171 "Could a £2-a-day basic income be the key to protecting rainforests?." Graeme Green, *The Guardian*, 22 August 2024. theguardian.com/environment/article/2024/aug/22/Indigenous-people-basic-income-protecting-rainforests-amazon-peru. Accessed 30 May 2025.

172 Matthew Owen, personal interview, 28 August 2024.

173 Brittany Christenson, personal interview, 4 October 2024.

174 Nicole Kelner, personal interview, 5 September 2024.

About the Author

Tasmin Lockwood is a journalist from the North East of England covering the intersection of technology and the climate crisis. She was previously a senior reporter at *Business Insider*, as part of its award-winning startups and venture capital team, where she covered climate technologies.

About the Inklings series

This book is part of 404 Ink's Inkling series which presents big ideas in pocket-sized books.

They are all available at 404ink.com/shop.

If you enjoyed this book, you may also enjoy these titles in the series:

How Does Change Happen? – Sam Gonçalves

Having a 'positive impact' in the world is often relegated to the 'personal', an individual endeavour. Gonçalves investigates that assumption and explores ways communities have resisted collectively, and fought against the individualising forces surrounding them.

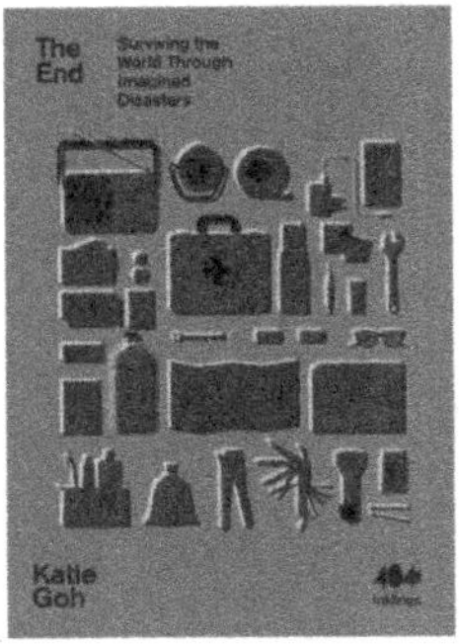

The End – Katie Goh

The word "apocalypse" has roots in ancient Greek, with apo ("off") and kalýptein ("cover") combining to form apokálypsis, meaning to uncover or reveal. In considering apocalypse fiction across culture and its role in how we manage, manifest and imagine social, economic and political crises, Goh navigates what this genre reveals about our contemporary anxieties, and why we turn to disaster time and again.

The Last Day Before Exile – Selin Bucak

Where displaced people are so often presented as "waves" of immigrants, Bucak shares the stories of immigrants who, during some of the hardest moments of their lives, must decide whether to stay or leave, tracing the steps of professionals who have moved from Gaza, Pakistan, Morocco, Iran, Afghanistan, Turkey, and Ukraine.